daybook, *n.* a book in which the events of the day are recorded; *specif.* a journal or diary

DAYBOOK
· · · · · · · · · ·
of Critical Reading and Writing

CONSULTING AUTHORS

FRAN CLAGGETT

LOUANN REID

RUTH VINZ

Great Source Education Group
a Houghton Mifflin Company
Wilmington, Massachusetts

www.greatsource.com

The Consulting Authors

Fran Claggett, currently an educational consultant for schools throughout the country and teacher at Sonoma State University, taught high school English for more than thirty years. She is author of several books, including *Drawing Your Own Conclusions: Graphic Strategies for Reading, Writing, and Thinking* (1992) and *A Measure of Success* (1996).

Louann Reid taught junior and senior high school English, speech, and drama for nineteen years and currently teaches courses for future English teachers at Colorado State University. Author of numerous articles and chapters, her first books were *Learning the Landscape* and *Recasting the Text* with Fran Claggett and Ruth Vinz (1996).

Ruth Vinz, currently a professor and director of English education at Teachers College, Columbia University, taught in secondary schools for twenty-three years. She is author of several books and numerous articles that discuss teaching and learning in the English classroom as well as a frequent presenter, consultant, and co-teacher in schools throughout the country.

International Standard Book Number: 0-669-46443-0

6 7 8 9 10 - RRDW - 04 03 02 01

3

4

5

6

| Focus/Strategy | Lesson | Author/Literature |

7

Angles of Literacy

Imagine that you come upon a brand-new product being demonstrated at the mall. You crane your neck. You may ask questions of people in the crowd. Pretty soon you move in for a closer look. You tilt your head this way and that, checking out the product from all angles. All the while, you're getting ideas about what the product is and how you might use it.

Literacy—understanding what you read—also involves looking from many angles. In a way, everything you read is like a new "product." What might it mean to you? How might it affect your life? That's what you're reading to find out. In this Daybook, you'll discover what it takes to be an active reader, involving yourself, your thoughts, and your feelings in your reading. The result can be surprising: unique insights that you might not otherwise have had.

One Becoming an Active Reader

To get involved in your reading, use your hands. Pick up a pen and mark up the page. Doodle in the margins. Invent your own code. You might underline parts you like and write ??? by parts that confuse you, xxx by parts that upset you, or !!! by parts that surprise you. You might draw circles or boxes around parts that seem important. Add comments, too. Notes like "Why?," "I don't think so," "True," or "I wonder . . ." are all part of active reading. In this *Daybook*, the response notes column by each selection gives you space to mark up what you read. Here's how one reader used it.

Response notes

sounds like a song—I like it.

This is like my bro, and his friend Dashaun.

I hope these guys are trying to be funny. . .

What's this about?

Understatement!

from *A Summer Life* by Gary Soto

In high school, girls were blossoms shaken from a tree and blooming with life. We didn't know how to talk to them, so we rehearsed by the school fountain. "Do you go to this school?" Scott asked, and I punched him in the arm. "Of course they do. Why else would they be here?"

I tried, "I walked by your house and saw that you have a palm tree. I have a palm tree. What a coincidence."

Scott tried: "It's cold for December."

I tried: "A June bug can live on a screen door for days."

Scott tried: "It rains a lot in April, but the funny thing is the rain is either very cold or very warm but never in between."

I tried: "My friend Tony said he would take the bullet for the president." ???

Scott tried: "Chicken is my favorite food."

We needed help.

Now read the first part of a short story by the same author. Mark it to show questions, ideas, and responses that it sparks in you.

"Seventh Grade" by Gary Soto

On the first day of school, Victor stood in line half an hour before he came to a wobbly card table. He was handed a packet of papers and a computer card on which he listed his one elective, French. He already spoke Spanish and English, but he thought someday he might travel to France, where it was cool; not like Fresno, where summer days reached 110 degrees in the shade. There were rivers in France, and huge churches, and fair-skinned people everywhere, the way there were brown people all around Victor.

Besides, Teresa, a girl he had liked since they were in catechism classes at Saint Theresa's, was taking French, too. With any luck they would be in the same class. Teresa is going to be my girl this year, he promised himself as he left the gym full of students in their new fall clothes. She was cute. And good at math, too, Victor thought as he walked down the hall to his homeroom. He ran into his friend, Michael Torres, by the water fountain that never turned off.

They shook hands, *raza*-style, and jerked their heads at one another in a *saludo de vato*. "How come you're making a face?" asked Victor.

"I ain't making a face, *ese*. This *is* my face." Michael said his face had changed during the summer. He had read a *GQ* magazine that his older brother borrowed from the Book Mobile and noticed that the male models all had the same look on their faces. They would stand, one arm around a beautiful woman, and *scowl*. They would sit at a pool, their rippled stomachs dark with shadow, and *scowl*. They would sit at dinner tables, cool drinks in their hands, and *scowl*.

"I think it works," Michael said. He scowled and let his upper lip quiver. His teeth showed along with the ferocity of his soul. "Belinda Reyes walked by a while ago and looked at me," he said.

Victor didn't say anything, though he thought his friend looked pretty strange. They talked about recent movies, baseball, their parents, and the horrors of picking grapes in order to buy their fall clothes. Picking grapes was like living in Siberia, except hot and more boring.

"What classes are you taking?" Michael said, scowling.

"French. How 'bout you?"

"Spanish. I ain't so good at it, even if I'm Mexican."

"I'm not either, but I'm better at it than math, that's for sure."

A tinny, three-beat bell propelled students to their homerooms. The two friends socked each other in the arm and went their ways, Victor thinking, man, that's weird. Michael thinks making a face makes him handsome.

"Seventh Grade" by Gary Soto

Response notes

On the way to his homeroom, Victor tried a scowl. He felt foolish, until out of the corner of his eye he saw a girl looking at him. Umm, he thought, maybe it does work. He scowled with greater conviction.

In homeroom, roll was taken, emergency cards were passed out, and they were given a bulletin to take home to their parents. The principal, Mr. Belton, spoke over the crackling loudspeaker, welcoming the students to a new year, new experiences, and new friendships. The students squirmed in their chairs and ignored him. They were anxious to go to first period. Victor sat calmly, thinking of Teresa, who sat two rows away, reading a paperback novel. This would be his lucky year. She was in his homeroom, and would probably be in his English and math classes. And, of course, French.

🖎 Does Victor's first day in seventh grade remind you of your own? Why, or why not?

12

🖎 Look again at your markings and response notes. Share them with some of your classmates. Compare your impressions of the story and the author. After your discussion, do a quickwrite to explore one of your questions about what you've read so far or about Gary Soto's writing.

Active readers get involved in their reading by marking selections with their own ideas, questions, and comments.

Two Story Connections

When you read a story, "step into" it by connecting it with your own experiences. If the story has a wild **character**, recall wild characters you've known. If it's set in a city, think about cities you've been in. If it focuses on a challenge, remember challenges you've faced. Even if the story includes experiences you've never had, try to imagine how they might feel to you. As you read the next part of "Seventh Grade," jot down memories and connections that the story triggers in you.

"Seventh Grade" (continued) by Gary Soto

Response notes

The bell rang for first period, and the students herded noisily through the door. Only Teresa lingered, talking with the homeroom teacher.

"So you think I should talk to Mrs. Gaines?" she asked the teacher. "She would know about ballet?"

"She would be a good bet," the teacher said. Then added "Or the gym teacher, Mrs. Garza."

Victor lingered, keeping his head down and staring at his desk. He wanted to leave when she did so he could bump into her and say something clever.

He watched her on the sly. As she turned to leave, he stood up and hurried to the door, where he managed to catch her eye. She smiled and said, "Hi, Victor."

He smiled back and said, "Yeah, that's me." His brown face blushed. Why hadn't he said, "Hi, Teresa," or "How was your summer?" or something nice?

As Teresa walked down the hall, Victor walked the other way, looking back, admiring how gracefully she walked, one foot in front of the other. So much for being in the same class, he thought. As he trudged to English, he practiced scowling.

In English they reviewed the parts of speech. Mr. Lucas, a portly man, waddled down the aisle, asking, "What is a noun?"

"A person, place, or thing," said the class in unison.

"Yes, now somebody give me an example of a person—you, Victor Rodriguez."

"Teresa," Victor said automatically. Some of the girls giggled. They knew he had a crush on Teresa. He felt himself blushing again.

"Correct," Mr. Lucas said. "Now provide me with a place."

Mr. Lucas called on a freckled kid who answered, "Teresa's house with a kitchen full of big brothers."

After English, Victor had math, his weakest subject. He sat in the back by the window, hoping that he would not be called on. Victor understood most of the problems, but some of the

13

stuff looked like the teacher made it up as she went along. It was confusing, like the inside of a watch.

After math he had a fifteen-minute break, then social studies, and, finally, lunch. He bought a tuna casserole with buttered rolls, some fruit cocktail, and milk. He sat with Michael, who practiced scowling between bites.

Girls walked by and looked at him.

"See what I mean, Vic?" Michael scowled. "They love it."

"Yeah, I guess so."

They ate slowly, Victor scanning the horizon for a glimpse of Teresa. He didn't see her. She must have brought lunch, he thought, and is eating outside. Victor scraped his plate and left Michael, who was busy scowling at a girl two tables away.

The small triangle-shaped campus bustled with students talking about their new classes. Everyone was in a sunny mood. Victor hurried to the bag lunch area, where he sat down and opened his math book. He moved his lips as if he were reading, but his mind was somewhere else. He raised his eyes slowly and looked around. No Teresa.

He lowered his eyes, pretending to study, then looked slowly to the left. No Teresa. He turned a page in the book and stared at some math problems that scared him because he knew he would have to do them eventually. He looked to the right. Still no sign of her. He stretched out lazily in an attempt to disguise his snooping.

Then he saw her. She was sitting with a girlfriend under a plum tree. Victor moved to a table near her and daydreamed about taking her to a movie. When the bell sounded, Teresa looked up, and their eyes met. She smiled sweetly and gathered her books. Her next class was French, same as Victor's.

●◆ **What do you think about Victor?**

14

●◆ What kinds of connections did you find between "Seventh Grade" and your own experiences? In a journal entry, explore one memory that "Seventh Grade" triggers in you.

15

When you connect your reading with your own experiences, you can get new insights about your reading and about yourself.

A perspective is a way of looking at things: a filter made of experiences, education, emotions, and dreams, through which a person sees the world. When you read, notice the author's perspective. Try looking through the author's eyes, and you'll be able to bring his or her message into clearer focus.

Gary Soto bases much of his writing on his childhood in the barrio of Fresno, in California's San Joaquin Valley. Below, in writings and interviews, he reflects on this perspective.

from an interview in *Contemporary Authors* by Jean W. Ross

"I like the youth in my poetry, sort of a craziness. For me that's really important. I don't want to take a dreary look at the world and then start writing."

from *A Fire in My Hands* by Gary Soto

"I tried to remain faithful to the common things of my childhood—dogs, alleys, my baseball mitt, curbs, and the fruit of the valley, especially the orange. I wanted to give these things life, to write so well that my poems would express their simple beauty."

from *California Childhood* by Gary Soto

"Childhood is not only place, but a response toward place. I'm speaking of fear and boredom, the sense of resignation in a poor family, the utter joy of jumping into cold river water, the loneliness of no girlfriend or boyfriend, envy of the rich in 'fresh' clothes, adolescent rebellion—human feelings that move beyond the borders of California to embrace all children."

Now read the rest of "Seventh Grade." Try looking through Soto's eyes, and notice parts of the story that illustrate Soto's statements about his perspective. Mark these places with a star.

"Seventh Grade" (continued) by Gary Soto

← Response notes

They were among the last students to arrive in class, so all the good desks in the back had already been taken. Victor was forced to sit near the front, a few desks away from Teresa, while Mr. Bueller wrote French words on the chalkboard. The bell rang, and Mr. Bueller wiped his hands, turned to the class, and said, "*Bonjour.*"

"*Bonjour,*" braved a few students.

"*Bonjour,*" Victor whispered. He wondered if Teresa heard him.

"Seventh Grade" (continued) by Gary Soto

Mr. Bueller said that if the students studied hard, at the end of the year they could go to France and be understood by the populace.

One kid raised his hand and asked, "What's 'populace'?"

"The people, the people of France."

Mr. Bueller asked if anyone knew French. Victor raised his hand, wanting to impress Teresa. The teacher beamed and said, "*Très bien. Parlez-vous français?*"

Victor didn't know what to say. The teacher wet his lips and asked something else in French. The room grew silent. Victor felt all eyes staring at him. He tried to bluff his way out by making noises that sounded French.

"La me vava me con le grandma," he said uncertainly.

Mr. Bueller, wrinkling his face in curiosity, asked him to speak up.

Great rosebushes of red bloomed on Victor's cheeks. A river of nervous sweat ran down his palms. He felt awful. Teresa sat a few desks away, no doubt thinking he was a fool. Without looking at Mr. Bueller, Victor mumbled, "Frenchie oh wewe gee in September."

Mr. Bueller asked Victor to repeat what he had said.

"Frenchie oh wewe gee in September," Victor repeated.

Mr. Bueller understood that the boy didn't know French and turned away. He walked to the blackboard and pointed to the words on the board with his steel-edged ruler.

"*Le bateau,*" he sang.

"*Le bateau,*" the students repeated.

"*Le bateau est sur l'eau,*" he sang.

"*Le bateau est sur l'eau.*"

Victor was too weak from failure to join the class. He stared at the board and wished he had taken Spanish, not French. Better yet, he wished he could start his life over. He had never been so embarrassed. He bit his thumb until he tore off a sliver of skin.

The bell sounded for fifth period, and Victor shot out of the room, avoiding the stares of the other kids, but had to return for his math book. He looked sheepishly at the teacher, who was erasing the board, then widened his eyes in terror at Teresa who stood in front of him. "I didn't know you knew French," she said. "That was good."

Mr. Bueller looked at Victor, and Victor looked back. Oh please, don't say anything, Victor pleaded with his eyes. I'll wash your car, mow your lawn, walk your dog—anything! I'll be your best student, and I'll clean your erasers after school.

Mr. Bueller shuffled through the papers on his desk. He smiled and hummed as he sat down to work. He remembered his college years when he dated a girlfriend in borrowed cars.

Response notes →

She thought he was rich because each time he picked her up, he had a different car. It was fun until he had spent all his money on her and had to write home to his parents because he was broke.

Victor couldn't stand to look at Teresa. He was sweaty with shame. "Yeah, well, I picked up a few things from movies and books and stuff like that." They left the class together. Teresa asked him if he would help her with her French.

"Sure, anytime," Victor said.

"I won't be bothering you, will I?"

"Oh no, I like being bothered."

"*Bonjour*," Teresa said, leaving him outside her next class. She smiled and pushed wisps of hair from her face.

"Yeah, right, *bonjour*," Victor said. He turned and headed to his class. The rosebushes of shame on his face became bouquets of love. Teresa is a great girl, he thought. And Mr. Bueller is a good guy.

He raced to metal shop. After metal shop there was biology, and after biology a long sprint to the public library, where he checked out three French textbooks.

He was going to like seventh grade.

◆ "Seventh Grade" is told from the perspective of Victor. Describe Victor's view of what happened in French class. Then describe the same events from the perspectives of Teresa and Mr. Bueller, the French teacher.

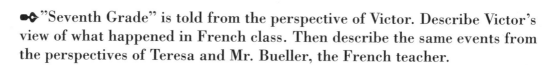

Victor	Teresa	Mr. Bueller

●◆ Gary Soto mentions four elements that make up his perspective:

• a youthful quality, "sort of a craziness"

• an upbeat approach, the opposite of "a dreary look at the world"

• attention to the "simple beauty" of commonplace things and events

• a focus on young people's emotions

●◆ With these four elements in mind, read back over "Seventh Grade." Then choose one element of Soto's perspective and explain where you recognize it in Soto's story.

19

●◆ What do you think is one message of "Seventh Grade"?

Noticing
an author's perspective
helps you to understand the
author's messages.

Gary Soto's first writings were poems. He recalls, "I once worked on a single fourteen-line poem for a week, changing verbs, reworking line breaks, cutting out unnecessary words." He goes on to explain, "Poetry is a concentrated form of writing; so much meaning is packed into such a little space. Therefore, each word in a poem is very important and is chosen very carefully to convey just the right meaning." To a degree, of course, the same is true in any type of writing. Authors craft their work carefully, choosing words to create strong images, to express ideas, and to spark feelings.

Gary Soto sees readers as his teammates: "You have to concentrate when you read a poem, just as you must concentrate when you're in the batter's box and your team needs you to bring in a player on second base." Take Soto's advice as you read his poem. Read it at least twice. Underline words or phrases that strike you as you read. Put a question mark next to anything that confuses you.

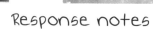

Response notes

Oranges
Gary Soto

The first time I walked
With a girl, I was twelve,
Cold, and weighted down
With two oranges in my jacket.
December. Frost cracking
Beneath my steps, my breath
Before me, then gone,
As I walked toward
Her house, the one whose
Porch light burned yellow
Night and day, in any weather.
A dog barked at me, until
She came out pulling
At her gloves, face bright
With rouge. I smiled,
Touched her shoulder, and led
Her down the street, across
A used car lot and a line
Of newly planted trees,
Until we were breathing
Before a drugstore. We
Entered, the tiny bell
Bringing a saleslady
Down a narrow aisle of goods.
I turned to the candies
Tiered like bleachers,

And asked what she wanted —
Light in her eyes, a smile
Starting at the corners
Of her mouth. I fingered
A nickel in my pocket,
And when she lifted a chocolate
That cost a dime,
I didn't say anything.
I took the nickel from
My pocket, then an orange,
And set them quietly on
The counter. When I looked up,
The lady's eyes met mine,
And held them, knowing
Very well what it was all
About.
        Outside,
A few cars hissing past,
Fog hanging like old
Coats between the trees.
I took my girl's hand
In mine for two blocks,
Then released it to let
Her unwrap the chocolate.
I peeled my orange
That was so bright against
The gray of December
That, from some distance,
Someone might have thought
I was making a fire in my hands.

Response notes

What do you like most—or least—about the poem?

21

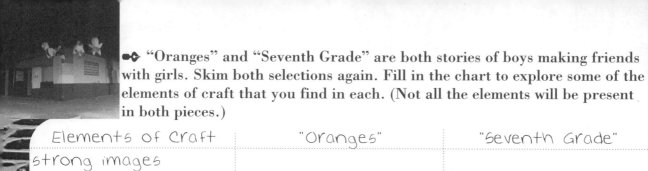

"Oranges" and "Seventh Grade" are both stories of boys making friends with girls. Skim both selections again. Fill in the chart to explore some of the elements of craft that you find in each. (Not all the elements will be present in both pieces.)

Elements of Craft	"Oranges"	"Seventh Grade"
strong images		
vivid descriptions of feelings		
humorous phrases or expressions		
realistic characterization		

●◆ Write a book-jacket blurb describing Gary Soto's craft. Use your chart and response notes for inspiration.

23

Active readers pay close attention to the way authors use words and sentences.

Five

Focus on the Writer

Like bits of shell on a beach, bits of authors' lives keep turning up in their works. Learning about an author's life can help you understand his or her writing. Remember that even a poem or story written in the first person (using *I*, *me*, and so on) is not necessarily autobiographical. However, a small kernel of real-life experience may provide a starting point for a piece that's primarily fictional.

The piece below *is* autobiographical. It describes Gary Soto's memories of picking grapes to earn money for school clothes. Read actively by marking it and adding your own comments and connections.

24

from *Living Up the Street* by Gary Soto

Response notes

I cut another bunch, then another, fighting the snap and whip of vines. After ten minutes of groping for grapes, my first pan brimmed with bunches. I poured them on the paper tray, which was bordered by a wooden frame that kept the grapes from rolling off, and they spilled like jewels from a pirate's chest. The tray was only half filled, so I hurried to jump under the vines and begin groping, cutting, and tugging at the grapes again. I emptied the pan, raked the grapes with my hands to make them look like they filled the tray, and jumped back under the vine on my knees. I tried to cut faster because Mother, in the next row, was slowly moving ahead. I peeked into her row and saw five trays gleaming in the early morning. I cut, pulled hard, and stopped to gather the grapes that missed the pan; already bored, I spat on a few to wash them before tossing them like popcorn into my mouth.

So it went. Two pans equaled one tray—or six cents. By lunchtime I had a trail of thirty-seven trays behind me while Mother had sixty or more. We met about halfway from our last trays, and I sat down with a grunt, knees wet from kneeling on dropped grapes. I washed my hands with the water from the jug, drying them on the inside of my shirt sleeve before I opened the paper bag for the first sandwich, which I gave to Mother. I dipped my hand in again to unwrap a sandwich without looking at it. I took a first bite and chewed it slowly for the tang of mustard. Eating in silence I looked straight ahead at the vines, and only when we were finished with cookies did we talk.

"Are you tired?" she asked.

"No, but I got a sliver from the frame," I told her. I showed her the web of skin between my thumb and index finger. She wrinkled her forehead but said it was nothing.

from *Living Up the Street* by Gary Soto

Response notes

"How many trays did you do?"

I looked straight ahead, not answering at first. I recounted in my mind the whole morning of bend, cut, pour again and again, before answering a feeble "thirty-seven." No elaboration, no detail. Without looking at me she told me how she had done field work in Texas and Michigan as a child. But I had a difficult time listening to her stories. I played with my grape knife, stabbing it into the ground, but stopped when Mother reminded me that I had better not lose it. I left the knife sticking up like a small, leafless plant. She then talked about school, the junior high I would be going to that fall, and then about Rick and Debra [Soto's brother and sister], how sorry they would be that they hadn't come out to pick grapes because they'd have no new clothes for the school year. She stopped talking when she peeked at her watch, a bandless one she kept in her pocket. She got up with an "*Ay, Dios*," and told me that we'd work until three, leaving me cutting figures in the sand with my knife and dreading the return to work.

Finally I rose and walked slowly back to where I had left off, again kneeling under the vine and fixing the pan under bunches of grapes. By that time, 11:30, the sun was over my shoulder and made me squint and think of the pool at the Y.M.C.A. where I was a summer member. I saw myself diving face first into the water and loving it. I saw myself gleaming like something new, at the edge of the pool. I had to daydream and keep my mind busy because boredom was a terror almost as awful as the work itself. My mind went dumb with stupid things, and I had to keep it moving with dreams of baseball and would-be girlfriends. I even sang, however softly, to keep my mind moving, my hands moving.

I worked less hurriedly and with less vision. I no longer saw that copper pot sitting squat on our stove or Mother waiting for it to whistle. The wardrobe that I imagined, crisp and bright in the closet, numbered only one pair of jeans and two shirts because, in half a day, six cents times thirty-seven trays was two dollars and twenty-two cents. It became clear to me. If I worked eight hours, I might make four dollars.

25

➡️ **What do you learn about Gary Soto through the experiences he describes?**

●◆ Skim "Seventh Grade" and "Oranges" again. ("Oranges" is not entirely autobiographical, even though the speaker is called *I*.) In these pieces, what elements do you notice from Soto's life, as he describes it in *Living Up the Street*?

"Seventh Grade"	"Oranges"

●◆ You understand more now about Gary Soto than you did when you began this unit. What do you think about Soto and his writing now? Write a paragraph explaining your thoughts.

Knowing the story of an author's life can give you insights into his or her writing.

Essentials of Reading

You read with more than your eyes. You also read with your mind. Just as your eyes scan words, recognizing their forms and patterns, your mind scans meaning, recognizing ideas, reasons, and possibilities. And just as you can train your eyes to identify words more easily, you can also train your mind to better understand what you read.

Each reader finds meaning in his or her own way. Some readers rely mostly on logic and reasoning. Others rely on the hunches and feelings that their reading sparks in them. Still others use a combination of approaches. As you work through the pages in this unit, you'll practice several techniques that can help you understand what you read—and you'll start to develop your own approach to reading for meaning.

One

One

One Thinking Ahead

As you read, your mind moves on ahead of you. You use reasoning to make **predictions** that you may not even be aware of—predictions about what might happen next in the selection, about what kind of person a character will turn out to be, or about how the story will end. When you notice your own predictions, you also notice how the author's reasoning compares to your own. You come to understand more about the selection—and about your own way of reading.

Read the selection below, from a diary kept by a girl just entering seventh grade. Her new school is called Junior High School (J.H.S.) 80. In your response notes, jot down any comments that occur to you as you read.

Response Notes

28

from *The Diary of Latoya Hunter* by Latoya Hunter

September 12, 1990
Dear Diary,

The dreaded Freshman Day is drawing near. I can see into the deranged minds of the 8th & 9th graders. They can't wait. I've heard rumors that they attack kids in the hall. I wonder if that could be true. Are they that cruel? I feel there will be a lot of fights between freshmen and seniors, I hope I won't be in any of them. The thing is, I know the kind of people they'll be aiming for. They are the quiet ones, the ones who aren't into the crowd, the kids who don't act like animals on the street. That's the kind of person I am. That's just how I am and how I'll leave J.H.S. 80. I'm not about to change to fit in their dead-in-an-alley-headed crowd. I intend to make something of myself. Life is too precious to waste.

September 13, 1990
Dear Diary,

Is it strange for someone to *want* to get sick so they can't leave their house for a day? Well, I do and you know why—it's Freshman's Day eve and tis not the season to be jolly. The older kids are really trying to make us believe like we're trespassing on their property. Well, it isn't theirs alone. If there is a special diary way of praying, pray I'll come home in one piece. I'll write to you tomorrow. If I survive.

How are Latoya Hunter's experiences in the first week of seventh grade similar to yours? How are they different?

●◆ In the space below, write your predictions about what will happen on Freshman Day.

I predict that. . .

●◆ Now check your predictions by reading more from Latoya's diary. Under response notes, write YES! by events that match your predictions. Mark # by events that are far from what you predicted.

from *The Diary of Latoya Hunter* by Latoya Hunter

September 14, 1990
Dear Diary,

   I can't believe I'm here writing to you with no scratches or bruises. I actually made it! Something must have snapped in the minds of the older kids. Maybe they remembered when they were freshmen themselves because there were only a few fights today. I witnessed one of them with a geeky looking boy who really fought back, badly as he did. They didn't really bother girls. I think that was decent of them. I'm really relieved as you may guess.

   In the morning, Mr. Gluck, the principal announced that if anyone even thought of touching us it would mean suspension. Maybe that was why this Freshman Day was so much calmer. Whatever reason why, I appreciate it.

   Well Diary, what I assume was the worst week of J.H. is over. I hope things will get better next week. It has to. It can't get any worse . . . or can it?

RESPONSE NOTES

●◆Do Latoya's experiences on Freshman Day surprise you? Why or why not?

_____

_____

_____

_____

_____

_____

_____

●◆Whether or not Latoya's experiences match your predictions, you had
good reasons for making them. What were some of your reasons for
predicting as you did?

_____

_____

_____

_____

_____

_____

_____

_____

Making
predictions and checking
them helps you get more out
of your reading.

Two
Adding Things Up

Making inferences, or "reading between the lines," can help you get the meaning of a selection. An **inference** is a reasonable guess, based on what the selection says. For example, read the following sentence: *At the cat show, I found myself surrounded by the horrid, smelly creatures.* Do you infer that the writer dislikes cats, or likes them?

Now, reread the selections from *The Diary of Latoya Hunter*, and make some inferences about what's important to Latoya. This time, in your response notes, put a check mark by any parts that show you Latoya's characteristics and interests.

●◆ Now imagine that you're a new friend in one of Latoya's classes, and she has told you the same things that she has written in her diary. Write a letter to another friend, describing Latoya. Include your inferences about the following questions:

- How important is school to Latoya?
- Does Latoya plan to work hard in school, or does she plan to take it easy?

Explain your inferences, and quote from Latoya's words to back them up.

Dear

Your friend,

Making inferences can deepen your insights into your reading.

Three

What's the Big Idea?

Everything you read has a **main idea**—the central thought that the writing explores. Once you know the main idea, the other parts of the piece fall into place for you, and the whole selection makes more sense. In **fiction**, the main idea is called the **theme**. It is usually a message or a lesson about life or about human beings. In **nonfiction**, the main idea is sometimes called a thesis. It may give information or an opinion. Often the main idea is not stated, but implied; then you need to make **inferences** to identify it. You'll know you've found the main idea when you can sum up, in one or two sentences, what the author's basic message seems to be.

In the article below, the main idea is not directly stated. As you read, use the response notes to jot down your inferences about what the main idea might be.

"Playgrounds of the Future" by Kendall Hamilton and Patricia King

←Response notes

32

On a sunny Sunday afternoon, seventh grader Josh Hartley is helping to build a wet-sand dam at Jack Fischer Park in his hometown of Campbell, Calif. A 6-year-old "reinforces" the dam with twigs. Another presses a button that floods a concrete channel with water, to test the structure's mettle. The barrier holds. "It's pretty cool," says Hartley. "You feel like you've accomplished something." The 13-year-old prefers this brand-new playground to more traditional ones, with their "rusty old stuff" that sheds paint chips and burns fingers after a few hours under the sun. The slides at Jack Fischer are plastic, and their impact zones are cushioned with special wood chips to ensure soft landings. That's important to Hartley, whose sister cut her chin when she fell from a climbing structure at another park. You won't find monkey bars or a Jungle Gym at Jack Fischer. And come the year 2000, you'll have a hard time finding them anywhere in California.

The state is the first in the country to mandate compliance with federal safety recommendations. Some long-beloved fixtures—monkey bars among them—will bite the dust, and others such as swings, slides and seesaws will have to be scaled down or modified. Traditionalists scoff at what they see as undue protectionism, but activists say changes are long overdue. About 150,000 children a year wind up in emergency rooms with playground injuries, and 15 or so die. Seymour Gold, professor of environmental planning at the University of California, Davis, says studies place playgrounds among the

"Playgrounds of the Future" by Kendall Hamilton and Patricia King

Response notes ↘

five greatest hazards to children in the nation. "That's serious, when you're up there with chain saws and ladders."

New and safer playgrounds are still evolving, but some trends are already clear. First, says designer Jay Beckwith, equipment will be lower to the ground. No more 20-foot-tall corkscrew slides. Merry-go-rounds, where kids kept whirling "until they threw up," could also trap children underneath, says Beckwith, so they're out. Old-style seesaws are giving way to spring-loaded ones so you can't "jump off and have your friend's eyeballs come out of his head." Heavy animal-shaped swings look like fun, but they routinely flatten passing toddlers. Even conventional swings are on the wane. "Swings are going to be very scarce, and high swings are going to be gone," says Beckwith. Mandated "fall zones" are so large and the surfacing required beneath them so costly that most parks don't have the space or money for more than a few. Writing a check for $10,000 to pad the area around two swings is no fun for civic officials.

But will the new playgrounds be any fun for kids? Designers are devising alternative fixtures, like Jack Fischer Park's water channel, but to some it just isn't the same. Marin County day-care assistant Kristen Eldridge, 25, has a "major problem" with the new rules. "I had seesaws and monkey bars when I grew up and I'm fine, and generations before us were fine," she says. "Parents are just getting too busy to take the time to watch their kids." Terry Norton, an irked mom who fired off an op-ed piece to the *San Francisco Examiner*, says the new rules will create "plastic-bubble childhoods for kids. Let them get out there and bang against hard things. It's reality."

But parents of children who bang against hard things often file lawsuits. It is this hazard, as much as nanny-minded legislators, that's driving the changes. Besides, "you're still going to break your arms and fingers," says Susan Goltsman, a Berkeley, Calif., playground designer. The new rules are aimed at eliminating deaths, she says, not minor injuries. And some of the new stuff is catching on. "Usually you get dirty and everything, but I think it's fun," says Josh Hartley of his park's water channel, which may not be dangerous but certainly offers a taste of reality. Budding civil engineers learn what it's like to work with bossy colleagues, and even the occasional conspiracy is hatched. "Let's go terrorize my brother," says one boy, proving that there are some childhood hazards that no amount of padding can eliminate.

◉ Would you prefer a playground like the one in Jack Fischer Park, or a more traditional one? Why?

◉ To find the main idea of "Playgrounds of the Future," use two steps:

1. Identify the topic of the piece. (The title and first paragraphs often give you clues about the topic.)

Topic:

2. Answer the question, "What about it?" (In other words, what do the authors say about the topic?)

What about it?

Now write a sentence that states the main idea of the article. The topic that you identified might form the subject of your sentence. Your answer to "What about it?" might form the rest of the sentence.

Identifying the main idea helps you to clarify what the selection is all about.

Four
In Your Opinion

Your good judgment is one of your best reading tools. It keeps you thinking independently about the things you read. Using your judgment, or evaluating, can involve asking yourself questions like the following ones:

- How do I feel about the people (or characters) in this piece?
- What might this information (or story) teach me?
- With which of this author's ideas do I agree most—and least?

Reread "Playgrounds of the Future." This time, in the response notes, write an *A* by each part that you agree with. Write a *D* by each part that you disagree with.

"Playgrounds of the Future" originally appeared in *Newsweek* magazine. Imagine that you are writing a letter to the editor of *Newsweek*. Explain your views about the article: Does it present both sides of the issue fairly? Do you think we need the planned changes in playgrounds? Why or why not?

Editor
Newsweek

Dear Editor,

Sincerely,

Evaluating
helps you think critically about
what you read.

Five
Reflecting

When you *reflect* on your reading, you explore your responses and the reasons for them. Reflecting helps you develop and understand your own tastes and interests. In reflecting, you might notice that parts of a selection remind you of your own experiences. You might ask questions about parts that puzzle you, or you might explore mental images that the selection sparks for you.

Read "A Time to Talk" once for meaning. Then read it a second time, stopping every two or three lines to reflect. See if you can create a mental picture of what the lines say. Put a star in the response notes by lines that give you a clear image. If a line, or part of a line, puzzles you, put a question mark by it in your response notes.

Response notes

36

A Time to Talk
Robert Frost

When a friend calls to me from the road
And slows his horse to a meaning walk,
I don't stand still and look around
On all the hills I haven't hoed,
And shout from where I am, "What is it?"
No, not as there is a time to talk.
I thrust my hoe in the mellow ground,
Blade-end up and five feet tall,
And plod: I go up to the stone wall
For a friendly visit.

●◆ Sketch or describe one image that the poem leaves in your mind.

➥ The speaker in the poem chooses a small incident to illustrate a big concept: the importance of friendship. Describe a small incident from your own daily life that might illustrate the same idea.

37

●◆After reflecting on "A Time to Talk," what does the poem mean to you?
How can you connect the poem's meaning to your own life?

Reflection
can help you to better
understand your reading and
yourself.

Essentials of Story

What's new and old at the same time? One answer is *a story*. A story—even a familiar one—is new each time it is told or read, as listeners or readers notice new things about it and gain new insights. At the same time, every story—even a just-written one—is old, in the sense that it shares basic elements with stories dating back to the dawn of human history. When you learn to recognize these basic story elements, you gain a deeper understanding of how all stories work. You can also better recognize the things that make each story unique. In the pages that follow, you'll deepen your understanding of stories as you examine five essential elements:

- setting
- character
- point of view
- plot
- theme

The **setting** of a story is the time and place of the action. Some stories are set in the past, others in the present or future. Some are set in real, or real-seeming, places; others are set in imaginary realms. Time of year, time of day, scenery, and social or cultural customs all work together to make up a setting. A story's setting helps to create the **mood**, or emotional atmosphere, that you sense as you read. When the description of the setting shifts, the mood may also shift.

In the following excerpt from *The Adventures of Tom Sawyer*, Tom and his friends, playing pirates, have spent the night on an uninhabited island in the Mississippi River. As you read, look for details of setting. Mark a *T* in your response notes for details of time, and a *P* for details of place.

response notes

from *The Adventures of Tom Sawyer* by Mark Twain

All nature was wide awake and stirring, now; long lances of sunlight pierced down through the dense foliage far and near, and a few butterflies came fluttering upon the scene.

Tom stirred up the other pirates and they all clattered away with a shout, and in a minute or two were stripped and chasing after and tumbling over each other in the shallow limpid water of the white sand bar. They felt no longing for the little village sleeping in the distance beyond the majestic waste of water. A vagrant current or a slight rise in the river had carried off their raft, but this only gratified them, since its going was something like burning the bridge between them and civilization.

They came back to the camp wonderfully refreshed, glad-hearted, and ravenous; and they soon had the campfire blazing up again. Huck found a spring of clear cold water close by, and the boys made cups of broad oak or hickory leaves and felt that water, sweetened with such a wildwood charm as that, would be a good enough substitute for coffee. While Joe was slicing bacon for breakfast, Tom and Huck asked him to hold on a minute; they stepped to a promising nook in the riverbank and threw in their lines; almost immediately they had reward. Joe had not had time to get impatient before they were back again with some handsome bass, a couple of sun perch, and a small catfish—provisions enough for quite a family. They fried the fish with the bacon, and were astonished, for no fish had ever seemed so delicious before. They did not know that the quicker a fresh-water fish is on the fire after he is caught the better he is; and they reflected little upon what a sauce open-air sleeping, open-air exercise, bathing, and a large ingredient of hunger makes, too.

➥Sketch the setting as you see it.

Now read on to see how Twain's description of setting changes as the day continues.

from ***The Adventures of Tom Sawyer*** by Mark Twain

RESPONSE NOTES

They found plenty of things to be delighted with, but nothing to be astonished at. They discovered that the island was about three miles long and a quarter of a mile wide, and that the shore it lay closest to was only separated from it by a narrow channel hardly two hundred yards wide. They took a swim about every hour, so it was close upon the middle of the afternoon when they got back to camp. They were too hungry to stop to fish, but they fared sumptuously upon cold ham and then threw themselves down in the shade to talk. But the talk soon began to drag, and then died. The stillness, the solemnity that brooded in the woods, and the sense of loneliness began to tell upon the spirits of the boys. They fell to thinking. A sort of undefined longing crept upon them. This took dim shape, presently—it was budding homesickness.

●◆In the "morning" space below, jot details about the forest that stand out for you in the first three paragraphs. In the "afternoon" space below, jot down details from the description of the forest in the last paragraph.

morning

afternoon

●◆How does the change in the way the forest setting is described reflect the change in mood?

The setting, or time and place of the action, can reflect mood or emotions in a story.

Two
The Cast

Characters are the people, animals, or other creatures carrying out the action in a story. Identifying characters is one of the first ways that readers connect with stories. Characters can be **static** (consistent and unchanging) or dynamic (inconsistent—as real-life people are—and capable of change). The main character, or protagonist, and other major characters are responsible for most of the action. Some stories also feature an **antagonist**—the main character's chief opponent. Minor characters play smaller roles.

Notice the many **details** that Mark Twain uses to introduce Huck Finn, a major character in *The Adventures of Tom Sawyer*. Use your response notes to comment on Huck.

---

from ***The Adventures of Tom Sawyer*** by Mark Twain

Huckleberry was cordially hated and dreaded by all the mothers of the town, because he was idle and lawless and vulgar and bad—and because all their children admired him so, and delighted in his forbidden society, and wished they dared to be like him. Tom was like the rest of the respectable boys, in that he envied Huckleberry his gaudy outcast condition and was under strict orders not to play with him. So he played with him every time he got a chance. Huckleberry was always dressed in the castoff clothes of full-grown men, and they were in perennial bloom and fluttering with rags. His hat was a vast ruin with a wide crescent lopped out of its brim; his coat, when he wore one, hung nearly to his heels and had the rearward buttons far down the back; but one suspender supported his trousers; the seat of the trousers bagged low and contained nothing; the fringed legs dragged in the dirt when not rolled up.

Huckleberry came and went at his own free will. He slept on doorsteps in fine weather and in empty hogsheads in wet; he did not have to go to school or to church, or call any being master or obey anybody; he could go fishing or swimming when and where he chose, and stay as long as it suited him; nobody forbade him to fight; he could sit up as late as he pleased; he was always the first boy that went barefoot in the spring and the last to resume leather in the fall; he never had to wash, nor put on clean clothes; he could swear wonderfully. In a word, everything that goes to make life precious that boy had. So thought every harrassed, hampered, respectable boy in St. Petersburg.

Tom hailed the romantic outcast:

"Hello, Huckleberry!"

"Hello, yourself, and see how you like it."

"What's that you got?"

Response notes

43

from **The Adventures of Tom Sawyer** by Mark Twain

"Dead cat."

"Lemme see him, Huck. My, he's pretty stiff. Where'd you get him?"

"Bought him off'n a boy."

"What did you give?"

"I give a blue ticket and a bladder that I got at the slaughterhouse."

"Where'd you get the blue ticket?"

"Bought it off'n Ben Rogers two weeks ago for a hoopstick."

"Say—what is dead cats good for, Huck?"

"Good for? Cure warts with."

"No! Is that so? I know something that's better."

"I bet you don't. What is it?"

🔖 Based on what you've read so far, do you think Huckleberry is a static character or a dynamic character? Explain.

....

....

....

....

🔖 Twain's description sheds light not only on the character of Huckleberry, but also on the character of Tom, who would be more like Huck if he could. In the spaces below, brainstorm 6–8 words that you might use to describe Huck and Tom. Then write one or two sentences that describe their differences as well as their similarities.

Tom	Huckleberry

One way to connect with a story is to analyze its characters.

Three The Vantage Point

Point of view is the vantage point from which a story is told. It lets the author offer insights into characters. If the narrator is one of the characters and calls himself or herself "I," the story is being told from the **first-person** point of view. If the narrator is not part of the story, the story is being told from the **third-person** point of view. A **limited** third-person narrator reveals the thoughts and feelings of only one character. An **omniscient** (all-knowing) third-person narrator reveals the thoughts and feelings of several characters.

In this selection, Hideyo Kawashima, a Japanese boy, is trying to escape Communist Korea during World War II. The Korean army has orders to kill the Japanese. Hideyo is found unconscious in the snow by a Korean family. The story is told from a **third-person limited** point of view. As you read, pay attention to the point of view. What are its advantages and disadvantages?

from *So Far from the Bamboo Grove*
by Yoko Kawashima Watkins

Response notes

"Is he a Japanese boy, Father?" asked Hee Wang.

"The way he carried his rucksack and the cherry flower emblem on the buttons of the uniform show he is Japanese," his father told him.

They took off leg wrappers, shoes, and wet socks. Hideyo wore four pairs of socks, half-frozen, and all the shirts he owned. Mrs. Kim wiped his body and massaged his chest.

"Look what I found," exclaimed Hee Wang. "A belly wrapper, with a notebook in it."

The notebook was a Japanese savings book. "What's his name, son?" asked Mr. Kim. Both of his boys could read the characters for "Kawashima." They hid the savings book and the contents of the rucksack, in case the Communist Army came to inspect the house.

Mrs. Kim put more wood in the clay firebox that heated the cooking vat and the rest of the house. While the men massaged Hideyo's legs and body, Mrs. Kim put crushed hot pepper in dry socks, put the socks on Hideyo's feet, and wrapped the feet in the little fur coat. More crushed dry pepper went onto Hideyo's chest, as the massage continued.

They put a nightshirt on him, covered him with a blanket, and tucked lots of straw over and around him. "He will be all right while we eat," Mr. Kim said.

As they ate, the farmer made his decision. "If he should die or if anyone finds out we have rescued a Japanese boy, we will

45

from *So Far from the Bamboo Grove*
by Yoko Kawashima Watkins

Response notes

be betrayed for prize money and executed. Listen, everyone. The boy is going to be my nephew. His parents were killed by Japanese and he has come to live with us. Do you understand? This way we are not in danger."

They ate quickly and then Mrs. Kim crushed garlic, added warm water, and tried to feed Hideyo as Mr. Kim forced open his mouth. His throat contracted—he swallowed. His feet were warming a little but his hands were ice-cold. Crushed pepper went into mittens for his hands.

Long after their sons had gone to bed Mr. and Mrs. Kim massaged Hideyo's body, kept water boiling for steam, and fed him garlic water with crushed hot peppers in it. Mr. Kim was feeding logs into the fire when his wife called out, "*Aboji* (Daddy)! He turned and groaned!" Mr. Kim rushed back and patted Hideyo's cheeks.

Honorable Brother returned to life, so tired that he could not move. He did not know where he was or who these people were. And where were his things? He was even fearful of being poisoned when the woman held a spoon to his lips. She tasted the pepper and garlic water to show him it was safe, and the hot mixture felt good to his stomach.

46

●◆ As you read this selection, which character did you find yourself caring most about? Explain.

●◆ Find out how changing the point of view can provide a different look at characters. Try rewriting part of the story using a third-person **omniscient** point of view. Imagine how Mr. and Mrs. Kim and their son Hee Wang might feel as they try to help Hideyo.

47

Point of view—the vantage point from which a story is told—helps to determine how much readers learn about each character.

Four
The Framework

A story's **plot** is its framework, the pattern of events in the story. Thinking about a story's plot gives you an overview that helps you understand the story. A plot usually revolves around a **conflict**—a struggle between characters, or between a character and some inner or outer force. Many plots have a five-part pattern:

CLIMAX
shows the story's high point, where action or suspense peaks

Rising Action
shows the development of the conflict

Falling Action
moves events toward their conclusion

Exposition
introduces the setting and characters

Resolution
offers explanations or hints about unanswered questions

Read "The Dinner Party" twice. The first time, read for pleasure. The second time, make notes that indicate where "the plot thickens"— that is, where you notice the action picking up or the suspense building.

Response notes

"The Dinner Party" by Mona Gardner

The country is India. A colonial official and his wife are giving a large dinner party. They are seated with their guests—army officers and government attachés with their wives, and a visiting American naturalist—in their spacious dining room, which has a bare marble floor, open rafters, and wide glass doors opening onto a veranda.

A spirited discussion springs up between a young girl who insists that women have outgrown the jumping-on-a-chair-at-the-sight-of-a-mouse era and a colonel who says that they haven't.

"A woman's unfailing reaction in any crisis," the colonel says, "is to scream. And while a man may feel like it, he has that ounce more of nerve control than a woman has. And that last ounce is what counts."

"The Dinner Party" by Mona Gardner

Response notes

The American does not join in the argument but watches the other guests. As he looks, he sees a strange expression come over the face of the hostess. She is staring straight ahead, her muscles contracting slightly. With a slight gesture she summons the servant standing behind her chair and whispers to him. The servant's eyes widen, and he quickly leaves the room.

Of the guests, none except the American notices this or sees the servant place a bowl of milk on the veranda just outside the open doors.

The American comes to with a start. In India, milk in a bowl means only one thing—bait for a snake. He realizes there must be a cobra in the room. He looks up at the rafters—the likeliest place—but they are bare. Three corners of the room are empty, and in the fourth the servants are waiting to serve the next course. There is only one place left—under the table.

His first impulse is to jump back and warn the others, but he knows the commotion would frighten the cobra into striking. He speaks quickly, the tone of his voice so arresting that it sobers everyone.

"I want to know just what control everyone at this table has. I will count to three hundred—that's five minutes—and not one of you is to move a muscle. Those who move will forfeit fifty rupees. Ready!"

The twenty people sit like stone images while he counts. He is saying ". . . two hundred and eighty . . ." when, out of the corner of his eye, he sees the cobra emerge and make for the bowl of milk. Screams ring out as he jumps to slam the veranda doors safely shut.

"You were right, Colonel!" the host exclaims. "A man has just shown us an example of perfect control."

"Just a minute," the American says, turning to his hostess. "Mrs. Wynnes, how did you know that cobra was in the room?"

A faint smile lights up the woman's face as she replies: "Because it was crawling across my foot."

49

●◆ Which event from the story can you see most clearly in your mind? Describe your mental picture.

→ Skim the story again, and look for the parts of the plot. (The first three paragraphs form the exposition; the last paragraph provides the resolution.) Within the rest of the story, which part do you consider to be the climax? Summarize it in the center area below. On either side, summarize the parts that you consider the rising action and the falling action.

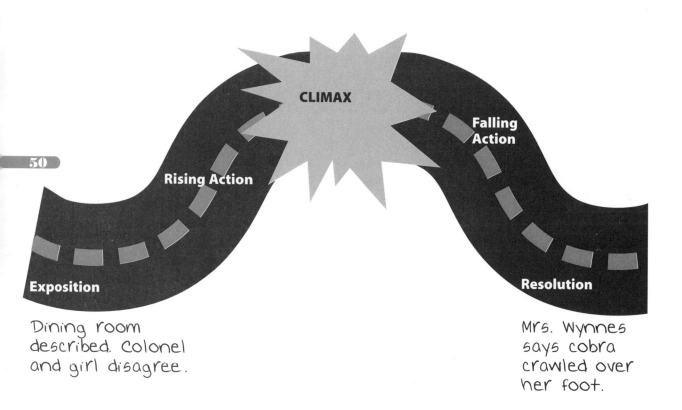

CLIMAX

Rising Action

Falling Action

Exposition

Dining room described. Colonel and girl disagree.

Resolution

Mrs. Wynnes says cobra crawled over her foot.

Examining a story's plot can give you a helpful overview of the events.

Five
The Message

A story's **theme** is its message about the world or about human beings. Exploring themes helps you understand authors' views on life. A theme is revealed by the events of the story. Many stories have more than one theme. Sometimes an author will state a theme directly, but more often, authors leave themes unstated, or implied, for readers to infer on their own. Readers' ideas about themes can vary. There is seldom just one "right" answer to the question, "What themes do you see in this story?"

To infer themes, you might:

- Ask yourself what lessons the main **characters** learn, or what lessons the main characters' experiences might teach you.

- Skim the story for sentences that offer comments on life, the world, or human nature. These comments, spoken by characters or by the **narrator**, may reflect the story's themes.

- Look at the title. Some titles provide clues about themes. If the title isn't much help, ask yourself what title you would give the story.

Read "The Dinner Party" once more, putting an asterisk (*) by parts that you find especially meaningful. Then, fill in the chart to show lessons that you think the characters learn by the end of "The Dinner Party."

Character	Lesson
the Colonel	
the girl	
the American	
Mrs. Wynnes	

●◆Imagine that Mona Gardner is dissatisfied with the title "The Dinner Party." She has asked you to suggest a new title. On the book cover, write a title reflecting one theme that you consider important in this story. On the lines, explain why you chose your title and what theme it reflects.

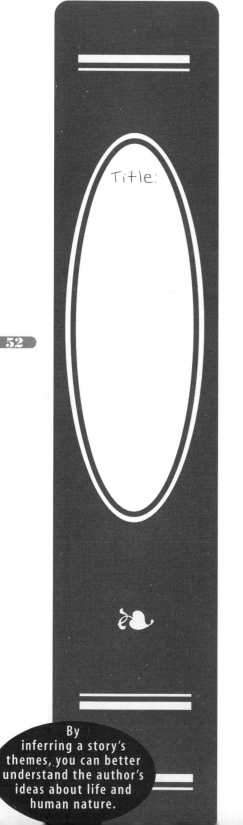

Title:

By inferring a story's themes, you can better understand the author's ideas about life and human nature.

Story and Genre

"A life is not important except in the impact it has on other lives."
—Jackie Robinson

When you hear "Jackie Robinson," whom do you picture? a gifted athlete who excelled in sports from tennis to football to golf? the first African American to play major league baseball? a man devoted to his family? a businessman? a tireless worker for civil rights? Jackie Robinson fulfilled all these roles and more. In this unit, you will explore different views of Jackie Robinson by reading several genres, or types of literary works, including a biography, autobiography, and poem. As you read, think about how each genre portrays Robinson in a different light. What are the strengths and limitations of each?

One An Outside Perspective

A biography is an account of someone's life, told from an outside **point of view**. Some biographers try to be impartial—they don't take a "side" and, instead, they just focus on the **facts** about the person. Other biographers clearly show their feelings about a subject. They might slant the facts (or omit some of them) to make their subjects look better or worse than they really are or were. A writer might even choose to portray only the incidents from a person's life that illustrate a certain point about him or her. As you read "Hero on the Ball Field," look for Robert Peterson's perspective on Jackie Robinson. Underline any opinions that you find. How does Peterson portray Robinson?

Response Notes

"Hero on the Ball Field" by Robert Peterson

As a baseball player, Jackie Robinson won over the fans, his teammates—and his own hot temper.

Robinson was a line-drive hitter, an acrobatic fielder and the best base runner of his time. He was also the first African-American player in the big leagues in this century.

In Robinson's rookie year, 1947, baseball topped the sports world. Pro football and basketball were far less popular 50 years ago.

It was a tough time to be black, and not just for baseball players. In Southern states, black kids went to separate schools. Black people had to ride in the backs of buses. There were even separate drinking fountains for blacks and whites. In the North, things were a little better, but not much. There had not been a black player in the major leagues in more than 60 years.

Blacks—even those good enough to play major-league baseball—had their own teams and leagues.

Jackie Robinson was a fiery competitor. "This guy didn't just come to play," an old baseball man once said. "He came to beat you!"

When the Brooklyn Dodgers signed Robinson, the club president, Branch Rickey, told Robinson he would have to curb his temper if he was abused or taunted by white players or fans. Rickey worried that if Robinson answered back, people who did not want blacks in baseball would say, "See, we told you blacks and whites should not compete."

Robinson asked, "Mr. Rickey, do you want a player who's afraid to fight back?"

"I want a player with guts enough *not* to fight back," Rickey said. "You've got to do this job with base hits and stolen bases and fielding ground balls, Jackie. Nothing else."

54

"Hero on the Ball Field" by Robert Peterson

Jackie Robinson was the loneliest man in baseball in 1947. During spring training a half-dozen Dodgers players said they would not play if he joined the team. Branch Rickey put down that mutiny with stern words. Soon most Dodgers warmed up to Robinson. They saw he was helping them win games.

Opponents were not so friendly. Some made it as tough as they could for the black pioneer. A few tried to spike Robinson as they crossed first base, Robinson's position that year, on a close play. He was hit by pitches nine times. Once he was kicked as he slid into second base.

Many players and fans screamed racial taunts at him.

"Plenty of times I wanted to haul off when somebody insulted me for the color of my skin," he said later.

Robinson was not even safe from hate at home. The mail brought letters threatening his life. Some letter writers said they would kidnap his infant son, Jackie Jr., or attack his wife.

Despite the great pressure on him, Robinson had a fine season. He batted .297, led the Dodgers in runs scored with 125 and hit 12 home runs. He led the league with 29 stolen bases. That may not seem like a lot today, but baseball was not a running game in 1947.

As a base runner, Robinson was constantly in motion. Pitchers worried more about him than the batter. Often the batter got a fat pitch to hit because the dancing Robinson distracted the pitcher.

Robinson sometimes "stole" bases after the ball was hit. He would race from first to third when the safe thing to do was stop at second.

But here is a fact that tells you how daring the muscular, pigeon-toed Robinson was on the bases: He stole home 19 times in his career, more than anyone since the early years of this century.

Fans—black and white—flocked to see Jackie Robinson play. In his first year, the Dodgers and four other National League teams set attendance records. He became a hero in black communities.

That year the Dodgers won the National League pennant but lost the World Series to the New York Yankees. Robinson was named National League Rookie of the Year.

Even before the 1947 season ended, Robinson's success paved the way for other black players. In July the Cleveland Indians signed Larry Doby, a slugging young outfielder, who became the first black player in the American League. A month later, pitcher Dan Bankhead, who had been with the Memphis Red Sox in the Negro American League, joined Robinson on the Dodgers.

55

HOME

TIME OUTS LEFT

BALL ON   DOW

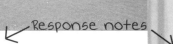

"Hero on the Ball Field" by Robert Peterson

Jackie Robinson's best position was second base, but he played all four infield positions and some in the outfield.

From 1949 to 1952 he was one of the two or three best players in baseball. In 1949 he led the National League in batting with a .342 average and in stolen bases with 37. He was third in triples and runs scored. That performance earned him the league's Most Valuable Player award.

Robinson retired from baseball in 1957, the year before the Dodgers moved to Los Angeles. Five years later he was elected to the Baseball Hall of Fame.

He became an outspoken leader in the fight for equality for black people. Jackie Robinson proved himself a hero off the baseball field as well as on.

●◆ Based on the article, what is your opinion of Jackie Robinson?

●◆ Look back at the opinions you underlined in the article. How does Robert Peterson feel about Jackie Robinson?

●◆Fill out the chart below to help you understand how Peterson uses incidents to express his views of Jackie Robinson.

Incident	What the Incident Reveals About Robinson
Robinson receives hate mail.	Robinson was able to perform well even under intense pressure and stress.

57

When you read a biography, consider why the author has chosen to describe certain events. Ask yourself, "What do these events tell me about the subject of the biography?"

Two In His Own Words

In an **autobiography,** a writer tells the story of his or her own life. Because the writer is telling about himself or herself, an autobiography usually isn't "just the facts." Instead, it gives a unique look at what the writer thinks and feels.

In *I Never Had It Made*, Jackie Robinson describes both his professional and personal life. The excerpt below describes a time during Robinson's first season with the Dodgers. Before these events, Robinson and his teammates had been heckled by the Philadelphia Phillies. As you read this excerpt, think about what the incident tells about Jackie Robinson. What can you learn from him that you wouldn't be able to discover in other sources?

Response notes

from *I Never Had It Made* by Jackie Robinson

That same spring the Benjamin Franklin Hotel in Philadelphia, where my teammates were quartered, refused to accommodate me. The Phillies heckled me a second time, mixing up race baiting with childish remarks and gestures that coincided with the threats that had been made. Some of those grown men sat in the dugout and pointed bats at me and made machine-gunlike noises. It was an incredibly childish display of bad will.

I was helped over these crises by the courage and decency of a teammate who could easily have been my enemy rather than my friend. Pee Wee Reese, the successful Dodger shortstop, was one of the most highly respected players in the major leagues. When I first joined the club, I was aware that there might well be a real reluctance on Reese's part to accept me as a teammate. He was from Ekron, Kentucky. Furthermore, it had been rumored that I might take over Reese's position on the team. Mischief-makers seeking to create trouble between us had tried to agitate Reese into regarding me as a threat—a black one at that. But Reese, from the time I joined Brooklyn, had demonstrated a totally fair attitude.

Reese told a sportswriter, some months after I became a Dodger, "When I first met Robinson in spring training, I figured, well, let me give this guy a chance. It may be he's just as good as I am. Frankly, I don't think I'd stand up under the kind of thing he's been subjected to as well as he has."

Reese's tolerant attitude of withholding judgment to see if I would make it was translated into positive support soon after we became teammates. In Boston during a period when the heckling pressure seemed unbearable, some of the Boston players began to heckle Reese. They were riding him about being a Southerner and playing ball with a black man. Pee Wee

from *I Never Had It Made* by Jackie Robinson

Response notes

didn't answer them. Without a glance in their direction, he left his position and walked over to me. He put his hand on my shoulder and began talking to me. His words weren't important. I don't even remember what he said. It was the gesture of comradeship and support that counted. As he stood talking with me with a friendly arm around my shoulder, he was saying loud and clear, "Yell. Heckle. Do anything you want. We came here to play baseball."

The jeering stopped, and a close and lasting friendship began between Reese and me.

●◆ What does Jackie Robinson reveal about himself and his attitude toward life in this excerpt?

59

●◆Imagine that you were a sportswriter covering this game. Write a short article about the incident Robinson describes. Remember that you are an outside observer.

Daily News

●◆ Use the Venn diagram to compare your "news" article with Robinson's autobiography. Focus on both the kinds of information revealed and the way that each is written (for example, its point of view).

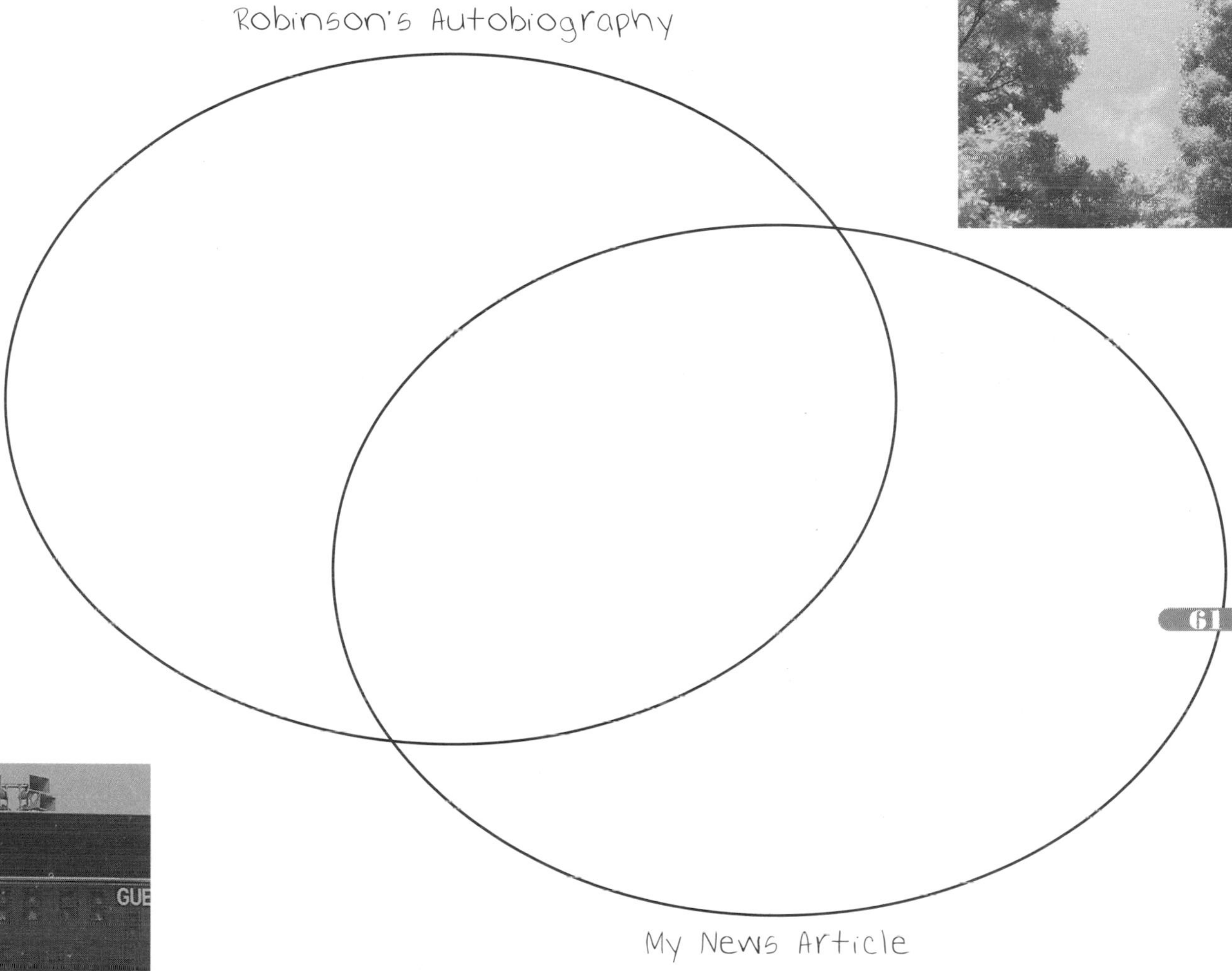

Robinson's Autobiography

My News Article

●◆ Use your Venn diagram to answer this question: What are the main advantages and disadvantages of autobiographical writing?

Advantages:

Disadvantages:

When you read an autobiography, consider how the writer's direct involvement might affect how he or she interprets what happened.

61

Three
Another Perspective

Do you think it would be difficult to write a **biography** about someone in your own family? Would you be able to be objective—in other words, could you tell just the **facts**? Or would your close relationship make you tell only the best things about your family member?

In her **autobiography**, *Stealing Home*, Jackie Robinson's daughter Sharon tells about her childhood in a famous family. In this excerpt, she recounts a dinner-table conversation. Jackie Robinson is talking about an incident in Little Rock, Arkansas, in 1957. When nine black teenagers began the court-ordered integration of schools, they faced jeers, taunts, and humiliation. Four of the children had spoken with Robinson about the ordeal. As you read this personal account, ask yourself, "What does Sharon Robinson reveal about herself and her father? What makes this account unique?"

← Response notes

from ***Stealing Home*** by Sharon Robinson

Without talking down to us, Dad used this opportunity to explain prejudice. Generally, he moved quietly around the house, but it was obvious that this situation had him worked up and he wanted my brothers and me to understand the situation.

"I suppose we all fear the unknown—the strange, the different. The natural fears of parents are made worse by ignorance, and unfortunately they pass them down to their children. In the process, the stories get more and more distorted and eventually become fact in the minds of the storyteller. The sad part for everyone is that prejudice prevents people from sharing talents which could benefit the whole community. The only way racial discrimination can have a hope of being erased is through exposure. The more people understand each other the less they will fear the differences."

"What did you say to the children, Daddy?" I asked, trying to picture their faces.

"Were they boys or girls?" David added.

"How old were they?" Jackie wanted to know.

Dad smiled and continued with the story of his phone conversation. He reminded us that the boys and girls were high school students. I felt somewhat relieved to know that they were much older than we were. I wondered how the children could possibly learn under such tremendous pressure.

I looked questioningly at Jackie, who was ten at the time, trying to picture him as a teenager going to high school. I figured my rebellious brother, Jackie Junior, would arrive at school and when he was told he couldn't go inside, he would

from **Stealing Home** by Sharon Robinson

Response notes

drop his books right in front of the soldiers (because he'd have to do something defiant), turn around, and go to the movies with his friends. I started to laugh at that image but then the sound of Dad's voice reminded me that we were discussing something serious. I took another bite of the baked chicken on my plate and chewed it, quietly listening to Dad.

"One of the girls I talked to this morning was named Gloria Ray and another was Minnie Brown. I told the girls that they were doing a tremendous job that made us swell up with pride. I wanted them to know that there were people throughout the country supporting them," Dad went on. "I couldn't believe Minnie's response. She said that they were following in my footsteps. Can you imagine?"

Dad's voice had faded. I had to strain to hear him. He was staring straight ahead not really focused on any one person, but I could still see the tears building in his eyes. I watched as he blinked several times. His expression said more than his words: a sadness because the children were so young; a pride in their courage and determination. I am sure that he also felt good playing a role, and grateful that the school experiences of his own children did not include such extreme displays of hatred.

I went to bed that night and dreamed of linking arms with Gloria, Minnie, Thelma, and Melba. We formed an impenetrable barrier. Our faces conveyed an unstoppable message. The National Guard offered no resistance. They parted their ranks and we entered Central High School. As far away as Arkansas was from Connecticut, I felt a bond with the children in Little Rock.

63

•❖ Do you think that Sharon Robinson's writing is objective? Why or why not?

....

....

....

....

....

➥ What does Sharon Robinson's account reveal about Jackie Robinson that the other two accounts (in Lessons One and Two) do not?

....

....

....

....

....

....

....

➥ You have read three different pieces of writing about Jackie Robinson. Brainstorm a list of Robinson's personal characteristics based on what you have learned from these pieces of writing. Then identify the source or sources for each characteristic by marking it **B** (Biography), **A** (Autobiography), or **PA** (Personal Account).

....

....

....

....

....

....

....

....

....

....

....

....

A personal account or memoir can provide readers with insights and details that may be absent from a more objective account.

Four A Poetic Portrait

You can tell a story about someone in many different ways. Some famous people are even the subjects of **poetry**. Poets, however, do not have as much "space" to tell someone's story. They need to convey a lot of information in a few lines. Because of this, poets often use images—words that paint a picture and evoke emotions as you read.

As you read Lucille Clifton's poem about Jackie Robinson, write in the response notes the images that you find in the poem. What words are you drawn to? Why?

Jackie Robinson
Lucille Clifton

ran against walls
without breaking.
in night games
was not foul
but, brave as a hit
over whitestone fences,
entered the conquering dark.

Response notes

65

To what does Clifton compare Robinson? What does Clifton's portrayal of Robinson suggest about him?

●◆ Try your hand at using Clifton's poetic style. Choose a person that you admire. Using figurative expressions, write a brief poem to show what makes that person special. Use Lucille Clifton's poem as a model by filling in each line beneath each of her lines.

Jackie Robinson

....

ran against walls

....

without breaking.

....

in night games

....

was not foul

....

but, brave as a hit

....

over whitestone fences,

....

entered the conquering dark.

....

Poets use figurative expressions and images to tell their own stories about people.

Five Thinking About Genres

Jackie Robinson—a baseball player, a friend, a father, a **symbol** of the struggle for racial equality. The pieces that you have read in this unit have shown you Jackie Robinson from all these perspectives through different **genres**. In the chart below, analyze the three genres. What are the strengths and weaknesses of each? As you complete the chart, think about how the **biography**, **autobiography**, personal account by Sharon Robinson, and poem all tell the same story, but in different ways.

Genre	Strengths	Limitations
biography		
autobiography		
personal account		
poem		

❧❖Create a picture-and-word collage that captures the many sides of Jackie Robinson. Be sure to include some ideas or images from each of the genres you read in this unit. You can write and draw or cut and paste your words and images in the space below.

68

Different genres can provide different perspectives on the same subject. Keep in mind the strengths and limitations of each as you read.

The Art of Language

A writer and a painter are both artists. While a painter expresses ideas and emotions by committing colors and images to canvas, a writer conveys feelings and ideas by using other kinds of tools. The "art" of language makes words become more than mere symbols on a page. As you read language that has been artfully written, you can feel the chill on a cold night when the fire goes out, understand a life-changing experience by seeing it through the eyes of a character, or gain new insight into something that you thought you already knew inside-out. In this unit, you'll learn more about techniques that writers use to turn language into art, including:

- using sensory language
- using imagery
- making comparisons with metaphors and similes
- using symbolism

One Show, Don't Tell

Sensory language is language that appeals to your senses: sight, sound, smell, taste, and touch. Imagine that you were describing a hot day at a swimming pool. You might use images like "the heat of the concrete baking the soles of your feet" or "the pounding beat of music blasting from a stereo."

When writers use sensory images, they give their work a "you are there" feeling. The reader becomes immersed in the picture that the writer-as-artist creates. As you read "knoxville, tennessee," highlight words and images that appeal to your senses.

Response notes

knoxville, tennessee
Nikki Giovanni

I always like summer
best
you can eat fresh corn
from daddy's garden
and okra
and greens
and cabbage
and lots of
barbecue
and buttermilk
and homemade ice-cream
at the church picnic
and listen to
gospel music
outside
at the church
homecoming
and go to the mountains with
your grandmother
and go barefooted
and be warm
all the time
not only when you go to bed
and sleep

70

●◆ What do you think of the poem?

●◆ What senses does Nikki Giovanni appeal to in her poem? Fill in the chart below, listing images from the poem that appeal to the five senses.

Sense   Images

Sight

Sound

Taste

Smell

Touch

●◆ Explore which images are most successful in helping you understand the poem.

With "knoxville, tennessee" as a model, use images to write a poem about your favorite season. Appeal to each of the five senses.

Two
Conveying Feelings

Imagery does more than just paint a picture with words; it also evokes strong feelings in readers. Imagine reading two **descriptions** of rain falling. One description uses images of drops puddling on the fresh green grass and the soft sound of rain tapping the window panes. The other describes the crash of thunder and the sight of whole sheets of rain bending trees to the ground. Both pieces depict a type of rain, but each conveys a different feeling: one of peace or contentment, the other of danger or fear.

When you read a piece of writing with imagery, think to yourself, "What images do I see? How do these images make me feel? What effect is the writer trying to achieve?" As you read "Graduation Morning," answer these questions in the response notes.

Graduation Morning
Pat Mora

She called him *Lucero*, morning star,
snared him with sweet coffee, pennies,
Mexican milk candy, brown bony hugs.

Through the years she'd cross the Rio
Grande to clean his mother's home. *"Lucero,
mi lucero,"* she'd cry, when she'd see him
running toward her in the morning,
when she pulled stubborn cactus thorns
from his small hands, when she found him
hiding in the creosote.

Though she's small and thin,
black sweater, black scarf,
the boy in the white graduation robe
easily finds her at the back of the cathedral
finds her amid the swirl of sparkling clothes
finds her eyes.

Tears slide down her wrinkled cheeks.
Her eyes, *luceros*, stroke his face.

Response notes

73

How do the images in the poem make you feel? Cite specific lines from the poem and describe the emotion each evokes.

Text Quotation	Emotion

Think of a feeling or emotion, such as sorrow, joy, excitement, or regret. Cut out images from magazines that communicate the emotion and paste or tape them into the *Daybook*. When you have finished, show your work to a partner. Can your partner tell what feeling you are trying to evoke?

Writers use imagery in their writing to evoke specific feelings in readers about the subjects and ideas of their works.

Three
Making Comparisons

The new pitcher's fastballs were rockets hurtling over home plate.

This sentence contains a **metaphor**—a comparison between two things that are not alike. A metaphor highlights the qualities of an object, person, or abstract idea (such as love). In this case, the writer uses a comparison to show how fast the ball went over the plate. When metaphors are well written, they reveal qualities in a way that is fresh and striking.

Some pieces of writing contain extended metaphors—an entire poem, for example, can be a single comparison between two things. In "Mother to Son," the speaker compares her life to a staircase. As you read the poem, use the response notes to jot down ways that the poem shows how life and a staircase are the same.

Mother to Son
Langston Hughes

Well, son, I'll tell you:
Life for me ain't been no crystal stair.
It's had tacks in it,
And splinters,
And boards torn up,
And places with no carpet on the floor—
Bare.
But all the time
I'se been a-climbin' on,
And reachin' landin's,
And turnin' corners,
And sometimes goin' in the dark
Where there ain't been no light.
So, boy, don't you turn back.
Don't you set down on the steps
'Cause you finds it kinder hard.
Don't you fall now—
For I'se still goin', honey,
I'se still climbin',
And life for me ain't been no crystal stair.

Response notes

75

●◆ For most people, the staircases that are their lives have had tacks, splinters, and twists and turns. To get a better idea of how the metaphor in the poem "works," pick three images from the poem. Write them in the first column of the chart. In the second column, explain how each line has been true of your "staircase" (or the staircase of someone you know).

Image from poem	My staircase
1.	
2.	
3.	

●◆ Create your own metaphor about life, love, or some other subject. Then write a short poem around it. The poem should clearly illustrate how the two things that the metaphor compares are alike.

Two things being compared: 1.

2.

Poem title:

When you read a metaphor, decide what qualities of an object, person, or idea the writer is trying to reveal through the comparison.

Four Another Way to Compare

The new pitcher's fastballs were like rockets hurtling over home plate.

Does this sentence seem familiar to you? Look closely—it is different from the **metaphor** in the last lesson. The new sentence includes a **simile,** another kind of comparison. Like a metaphor, a simile compares two unlike things. And like metaphors, similes highlight the qualities of an object, person, or idea. But a simile uses the word *like* or *as* to make the comparison.

Writers use similes to help you see something in a new and different light. After you've read "Birthday Box" once, reread it and circle any similes you find. Write what the author is comparing in the response notes. Be careful, though—not every sentence with the word *like* or *as* is a simile.

"Birthday Box" by Jane Yolen

Response notes

I was ten years old when my mother died. Ten years old on that very day. Still she gave me a party of sorts. Sick as she was, Mama had seen to it, organizing it at the hospital. She made sure the doctors and nurses all brought me presents. We were good friends with them all by that time, because Mama had been in the hospital for so long.

The head nurse, V. Louise Higgins (I never did know what that *V* stood for), gave me a little box, which was sort of funny because she was the biggest of all the nurses there. I mean she was tremendous. And she was the only one who insisted on wearing all white. Mama had called her the great white shark when she was first admitted, only not to V. Louise's face. "All those needles," Mama had said. "Like teeth." But V. Louise was sweet, not sharklike at all, and she'd been so gentle with Mama.

I opened the little present first. It was a fountain pen, a real one, not a fake one like you get at Kmart.

"Now you can write beautiful stories, Katie," V. Louise said to me.

I didn't say that stories come out of your head, not out of a pen. That wouldn't have been polite, and Mama—even sick—was real big on politeness.

"Thanks, V. Louise," I said.

The Stardust Twins—which is what Mama called Patty and Tracey-lynn because they reminded her of dancers in an old-fashioned ballroom—gave me a present together. It was a diary and had a picture of a little girl in pink, reading in a garden swing. A little young for me, a little too cute. I mean, I read Stephen King and want to write like him. But as Mama always reminded me whenever Dad finally remembered to send me something, it was the thought that counted, not the actual gift.

"It's great," I told them. "I'll write in it with my new pen." And I wrote my name on the first page just to show them I meant it.

They hugged me and winked at Mama. She tried to wink back but was just too tired and shut both her eyes instead.

Lily, who is from Jamaica, had baked me some sweet bread. Mary Margaret gave me a gold cross blessed by the pope, which I put on even though Mama and I weren't churchgoers. That was Dad's thing.

Then Dr. Dann, the intern who was on days, and Dr. Pucci, the oncologist (which is the fancy name for a cancer doctor), gave me a big box filled to the top with little presents, each wrapped up individually. All things they knew I'd love—paperback books and writing paper and erasers with funny animal heads and colored paper clips and a rubber stamp that printed FROM KATIE'S DESK and other stuff. They must have raided a stationery store.

There was one box, though, they held out till the end. It was about the size of a large top hat. The paper was deep blue and covered with stars; not fake stars but real stars, I mean, like a map of the night sky. The ribbon was two shades of blue with silver threads running through. There was no name on the card.

"Who's it from?" I asked.

None of the nurses answered, and the doctors both suddenly were studying the ceiling tiles with the kind of intensity they usually saved for X rays. No one spoke. In fact the only sound for the longest time was Mama's breathing machine going in and out and in and out. It was a harsh, horrible, insistent sound, and usually I talked and talked to cover up the noise. But I was waiting for someone to tell me.

At last V. Louise said, "It's from your mama, Katie. She told us what she wanted. And where to get it."

I turned and looked at Mama then, and her eyes were open again. Funny, but sickness had made her even more beautiful than good health had. Her skin was like that old paper, the kind they used to write on with quill pens, and stretched out over her bones so she looked like a model. Her eyes, which had been a deep, brilliant blue, were now like the fall sky, bleached and softened. She was like a faded photograph of herself. She smiled a very small smile at me. I knew it was an effort.

"It's you," she mouthed. I read her lips. I had gotten real good at that. I thought she meant it was a present for me.

"Of course it is," I said cheerfully. I had gotten good at that, too, being cheerful when I didn't feel like it. "Of course it is."

"Birthday Box" by Jane Yolen

Response notes

I took the paper off the box carefully, not tearing it but folding it into a tidy packet. I twisted the ribbons around my hand and then put them on the pillow by her hand. It made the stark white hospital bed look almost festive.

Under the wrapping, the box was beautiful itself. It was made of a heavy cardboard and covered with a linen material that had a pattern of cloud-filled skies.

I opened the box slowly and . . .

"It's empty," I said. "Is this a joke?" I turned to ask Mama, but she was gone. I mean, her body was there, but she wasn't. It was as if she was as empty as the box.

Dr. Pucci leaned over her and listened with a stethoscope, then almost absently patted Mama's head. Then, with infinite care, V. Louise closed Mama's eyes, ran her hand across Mama's cheek, and turned off the breathing machine.

"Mama!" I cried. And to the nurses and doctors, I screamed, "Do something!" And because the room had suddenly become so silent, my voice echoed back at me. "Mama, do something."

I cried steadily for, I think, a week. Then I cried at night for a couple of months. And then for about a year I cried at anniversaries, like Mama's birthday or mine, at Thanksgiving, on Mother's Day. I stopped writing. I stopped reading except for school assignments. I was pretty mean to my half brothers and totally rotten to my stepmother and Dad. I felt empty and angry, and they all left me pretty much alone.

And then one night, right after my first birthday without Mama, I woke up remembering how she had said, "It's you." Not, "It's for you," just "It's you." Now Mama had been a high school English teacher and a writer herself. She'd had poems published in little magazines. She didn't use words carelessly. In the end she could hardly use any words at all. So—I asked myself in that dark room—why had she said, "It's you"? Why were they the very last words she had ever said to me, forced out with her last breath?

I turned on the bedside light and got out of bed. The room was full of shadows, not all of them real.

Pulling the desk chair over to my closet, I climbed up and felt along the top shelf, and against the back wall, there was the birthday box, just where I had thrown it the day I had moved in with my dad.

I pulled it down and opened it. It was as empty as the day I had put it away.

"It's you," I whispered to the box.

And then suddenly I knew.

Mama had meant *I* was the box, solid and sturdy, maybe

Response notes

even beautiful or at least interesting on the outside. But I had to fill up the box to make it all it could be. And I had to fill me up as well. She had guessed what might happen to me, had told me in a subtle way. In the two words she could manage.

I stopped crying and got some paper out of the desk drawer. I got out my fountain pen. I started writing, and I haven't stopped since. The first thing I wrote was about that birthday. I put it in the box, and pretty soon that box was overflowing with stories. And poems. And memories.

And so was I.

And so was I.

⬤◆Look back at the similes about Katie's mother. What do the similes reveal about Katie's feelings toward her mother?

Choose a family member or friend who means a lot to you. Write a character sketch of him or her. Use similes in your character sketch that show what the person is like and reveal what makes him or her so special to you. Try to use comparisons that are fresh and interesting.

My character sketch is about

Writers use similes to give readers fresh insight into the qualities of objects, people, and ideas.

Five Symbols

A picture on a door tells you which bathroom to use. A slash mark across an object says "Don't do this." What do these "pictures" have in common? They are both symbols. **Symbols** are objects, people, or actions that can stand for something else. An "S" with two vertical lines through it, for example, means "dollars." A dove is a common symbol for peace.

➥ In "Birthday Box," one of the first clues that the box is a symbol is when Katie's mother says, "It's you." What does she mean when she says that? What do you think the box symbolizes? Why?

....

....

....

....

....

82

....

....

➥ Now think of an object that symbolizes *you*. Draw a picture of the object for a museum display of your life. Under the picture, write a short caption that tells how the object symbolizes you.

Writers use symbols to reveal qualities about objects, people, or ideas.

83

The Art of Argument

Imagine yourself standing at a microphone, facing a crowd of angry students. As student body president, it's your job to convince the group that the district's plan for year-round school is a great idea. What would you say? You'd need a really persuasive argument to convince the students to share your perspective.

A well-constructed argument is a work of art, just as a landscape or still-life painting is a work of art. When an argument is effective, you can't help but consider the viewpoint of the person presenting the argument. How do writers construct persuasive arguments? They combine a strong thesis, adequate support, and an understanding of both the opposition and the audience. Knowing how to blend these elements in a persuasive way is part of the art of argument.

One Thinking About Thesis

The purpose of an argument is to persuade others to share your viewpoint—that is, your perspective on a topic. If you want your argument to be effective, you need a clear and memorable thesis statement. The thesis statement is the main idea of an argument. It is the sentence or two in which the author states his or her **viewpoint**.

To find the thesis statement, begin by deciding what issue or topic the author is writing about. Once you know what the issue is, ask yourself two questions:

- What is the author's viewpoint on this issue or topic?
- Where does he or she state that viewpoint?

Once you've found the exact spot where the author states his or her viewpoint, you've found the thesis statement. For an example, read this opening paragraph of an argument. Notice the author's thesis statement.

> Everywhere you look in Indiana these days, you can see construction companies bulldozing farmland in order to build houses. New developments are popping up as fast as corn in the summer heat. Soon there will be no farmland left at all. This is a terrible crisis. We need to preserve our farmland in the same way that we preserve other national treasures like the Grand Canyon and Yosemite Park. The time to act is now!

thesis statement

84

Now read the following excerpt from Richard Carlson's nonfiction book, *Don't Sweat the Small Stuff*. As you read, circle the words and phrases that reveal Carlson's topic. When you come across his thesis statement, underline it.

Response Notes

"Practice Random Acts of Kindness"
from ***Don't Sweat the Small Stuff*** by Richard Carlson

There is a bumper sticker that has been out for some time now. You can see it on cars all across the nation (in fact, I have one on my own car). It says, "Practice Random Acts of Kindness and Senseless Acts of Beauty." I have no idea who thought of this idea, but I've never seen a more important message on a car in front of me. Practicing random kindness is an effective way to get in touch with the joy of giving without expecting anything in return. It's best practiced without letting anyone know what you are doing.

There are five toll bridges in the San Francisco Bay Area. A while back, some people began paying the tolls of the cars immediately behind them. The drivers would drive to the toll window, and pull out their dollar bill, only to be informed, "Your toll has been paid by the car ahead of you." This is an example of a spontaneous, random gift, something given

"Practice Random Acts of Kindness"
from *Don't Sweat the Small Stuff* by Richard Carlson

without expectation of or demand for anything in return. You can imagine the impact that tiny gift had on the driver of the car! Perhaps it encouraged him to be a nicer person that day. Often a single act of kindness sets a series of kind acts in motion.

There is no prescription for how to practice random kindness. It comes from the heart. Your gift might be to pick up litter in your neighborhood, make an anonymous contribution to a charity, send some cash in an unmarked envelope to make someone experiencing financial stress breathe a little easier, save an animal by bringing it to an animal rescue agency, or get a volunteer position feeding hungry people at a church or shelter. You may want to do all these things, and more. The point is, giving is fun and it doesn't have to be expensive.

Perhaps the greatest reason to practice random kindness is that it brings great contentment into your life. Each act of kindness rewards you with positive feelings and reminds you of the important aspects of life—service, kindness, and love. If we all do our own part, pretty soon we will live in a nicer world.

85

●◆ Think about Carlson's argument. Do you agree with his thesis? Why or why not?

....

....

....

....

....

....

....

....

....

....

....

....

●◆ Spend a day testing Carlson's thesis. Practice "random acts of kindness and senseless acts of beauty" everywhere you go. Keep a record of your "acts" in your *Daybook*. Also note whether or not each act helped you "get in touch with the joy of giving."

Testing Carlson's Thesis

My random acts of kindness	My senseless acts of beauty	Did the acts help me get in touch with the joy of giving?

To be effective, an argument's thesis statement should be clear and memorable.

Two Supporting Your Thesis

Every argument needs support. *Support* is the series of **details** that persuades readers to accept the thesis. If you were to put the relationship between the thesis statement and its support in mathematical terms, the equation would look like this:

$$\frac{\text{thesis statement} + 2 \text{ to } 3 \text{ pieces of support}}{\text{an effective argument}}$$

One way of supporting an argument is with **facts**, **figures**, and **statistics**. Another way of supporting an argument is with *anecdotal support*—that is, telling a story or giving an example that proves the point you want to make. These stories or examples can come from a book, magazine, or newspaper you've read, from your own life, or even from something you've overheard in the school lunch line.

Return to "Practice Random Acts of Kindness" with a pen in hand. What stories and examples does Carlson use to support his argument? Draw a star in the margin next to each piece of anecdotal support.

◆ Now create a plan for your own persuasive piece. Working in a small group, brainstorm a list of issues related to your school or community.

87

Group's list of issues:

....

....

....

....

....

....

....

....

....

●◆ Choose one of the topics from your group's list and then write an opinion about it that could be used as the basis for an argument. Next, think of two or three pieces of anecdotal support for your argument. Use this form to plan your argument.

Topic:

My Opinion about the topic:

Anecdotal support for my argument:

1.

88

2.

3.

One way of supporting an argument is with anecdotes and examples.

Three
Using Facts and Statistics

Persuasive writers know that offering a story or example that relates to their thesis statement is one good way to support an argument. An equally effective way of supporting an argument is to use numbers, figures, statistics, charts, graphs, or any other information that can be proven true.

Read this excerpt from "The Eternal Frontier," an essay written by Louis L'Amour, a novelist known for his tales of the Wild West. As you read, write *fact* in the margin when L'Amour supports his thesis with a fact or figure. If you're not sure whether something is a fact or an opinion, put a question mark in the margin. Underline L'Amour's thesis statement as well.

from **"The Eternal Frontier"** by Louis L'Amour

Response notes

The question I am most often asked is, "Where is the frontier now?"

The answer should be obvious. Our frontier lies in outer space.

The moon, the asteroids, the planets, these are mere stepping stones, where we will test ourselves, learn needful lessons, and grow in knowledge before we attempt those frontiers beyond our solar system. Outer space is a frontier without end, the eternal frontier, an everlasting challenge to explorers not alone of other planets and other solar systems but also of the mind of man.

All that has gone before was preliminary. We have been preparing ourselves mentally for what lies ahead. Many problems remain, but if we can avoid a devastating war we shall move with a rapidity scarcely to be believed. In the past seventy years we have developed the automobile, radio, television, transcontinental and transoceanic flight, and the electrification of the country, among a multitude of other such developments. In 1900 there were 144 miles of surfaced road in the United States. Now there are over 3,000,000. Paved roads and the development of the automobile have gone hand in hand, the automobile being civilized man's antidote to overpopulation.

What is needed now is leaders with perspective; we need leadership on a thousand fronts, but they must be men and women who can take the long view and help to shape the outlines of our future. There will always be the nay-sayers, those who cling to our lovely green planet as a baby clings to its mother, but there will be others like those who have taken us this far along the path to a limitless future.

from **"The Eternal Frontier"** by Louis L'Amour

We are a people born to the frontier. It has been a part of our thinking, waking, and sleeping since men first landed on this continent. The frontier is the line that separates the known from the unknown wherever it may be, and we have a driving need to see what lies beyond. It was this that brought people to America, no matter what excuses they may have given themselves or others.

Freedom of religion, some said, and the need for land, a better future for their children, the lust for gold, or the desire to escape class restrictions—all these reasons were given. The fact remains that many, suffering from the same needs and restrictions, did not come.

Why then did some cross the ocean to America and not others? Of course, all who felt that urge did not come to America; some went to India, Africa, Australia, New Zealand, or elsewhere. Those who did come to America began almost at once to push inland, challenging the unknown, daring to go beyond the thin line that divides the known and the unknown. Many had, after landing from the old country, developed good farms or successful businesses; they had become people of standing in their communities. Why then did they move on, leaving all behind?

I believe it to be something buried in their genes, some inherited trait, perhaps something essential to the survival of the species.

They went to the edge of the mountains; then they crossed the mountains and found their way through impassable forests to the Mississippi. After that the Great Plains, the Rocky Mountains, and on to Oregon and California. They trapped fur, traded with Indians, hunted buffalo, ranched with cattle or sheep, built towns, and farmed. Yet the genes lay buried within them, and after a few months, a few years, they moved on.

Each science has its own frontiers, and the future of our nation and the world lies in research and development, in probing what lies beyond.

A few years ago we moved into outer space. We landed men on the moon; we sent a vehicle beyond the limits of the solar system, a vehicle still moving farther and farther into that limitless distance. If our world were to die tomorrow, that tiny vehicle would go on and on forever, carrying its mighty message to the stars. Out there, someone, sometime, would know that once we existed, that we had the vision and we made the effort. Mankind is not bound by its atmospheric envelope or by its gravitational field, nor is the mind of man bound by any limits at all.

●✦ Do you agree with L'Amour's thesis that space is the final frontier? Do you think L'Amour did a good job supporting his thesis with facts and statistics? Explain your answer.

....

....

....

....

●✦ Imagine you've been asked to support the argument that computers and the Internet are the final frontiers. What facts, figures, anecdotes, or examples might you present? Make a list of possible sources to support your opinion.

1. I might start out by thumbing through my Dad's computer magazines. What information do they have about interest in the Internet?

2.

3.

4.

5.

When you read an argument, look for facts and figures that support the author's perspective.

Four. Refute Opposition

There are two sides to every argument. You can strengthen your side of an argument by explaining why you disagree with the other side. This is called **refuting opposing arguments**. Refuting an opposing argument is like saying to your audience: "Look, I understand your viewpoint, but I disagree with it because of *a*, *b*, and *c*." When you refute the opposition, you deal with any objections to your argument—before the objections are even raised.

Read the speech that follows. It was given by an African-American woman named Sojourner Truth at a women's rights convention in 1851. Circle the places in the speech where Truth recognizes, then refutes, opposing arguments. How does this make her argument more persuasive? Be sure to watch for and underline her thesis statement.

←Response notes

"Ain't I a Woman?" by Sojourner Truth

Well, children, where there is so much racket there must be something out of kilter. I think that 'twixt the Negroes of the South and the women at the North, all talking about rights, the white men will be in a fix pretty soon. But what's all this here talking about? That man over there says that women need to be helped into carriages, and lifted over ditches, and to have the best place everywhere. Nobody ever helps me into carriages, or over mud-puddles, or gives me any best place! And ain't I a woman? Look at me! Look at my arm! I have plowed and planted, and gathered into barns, and no man could head me! And ain't I a woman? I could work as much and eat as much as a man—when I could get it—and bear the lash as well! And ain't I a woman? I have borne thirteen children, and seen them most all sold off to slavery, and when I cried out with my mother's grief, none but Jesus heard! And ain't I a woman?

Then they talk about this thing in the head; what's this they call it? ["Intellect," someone in the audience whispers.] That's it, honey. What's that got to do with women's rights or Negro's rights? If my cup won't hold but a pint, and yours holds a quart, wouldn't you be mean not to let me have my little half-measure full?

Then that little man in black there, he says women can't have as much rights as men, 'cause Christ wasn't a woman! Where did your Christ come from? Where did your Christ come from? From god and a woman! Man had nothing to do with him.

If the first woman God ever made was strong enough to turn the world upside down all alone, these women together ought to be able to turn it back, and get it right side up again!

"Ain't I a Woman?" by Sojourner Truth

And now they is asking to do it, the men better let them. Obliged to you for hearing me, and now old Sojourner ain't got nothing more to say.

Response notes

🖛 Think about Sojourner Truth's argument. Then use the chart below to track the ways she refutes her opposition. Add three or four points to the chart and explain how Sojourner refutes each one.

What the opposition says	Sojourner Truth's response
Women need to be taken care of.	"Nobody ever helps me into carriages, or over mud-puddles, or gives me any best place! And ain't I a woman?"
Women are weak.	

●◆The issue of women's rights is obviously a topic Sojourner Truth felt strongly about. What issues are important to you? Choose a topic you feel strongly about. List three opposing arguments. Then explain how you would refute each.

Topic:

My opinion or thesis:

Opposing Arguments	How I'd Refute Opposition

By refuting the opposition, you can give additional strength to your side of the argument.

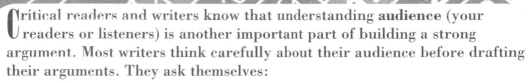

Five

Understanding Audience

Critical readers and writers know that understanding **audience** (your readers or listeners) is another important part of building a strong argument. Most writers think carefully about their audience before drafting their arguments. They ask themselves:

• What are the needs and perspectives of my audience?

• How are those needs and perspectives different from mine?

• What response do I want from my audience?

• How can I get my audience to agree with my thesis?

Reread the selections in this unit, and circle any words or phrases that give you clues about audience. Do L'Amour, Carlson, and Truth all seem aware of the needs and perspectives of their audience? Explain.

L'Amour	Carlson	Truth

●◆ Now plan an argument of your own. (Choose a topic that is different from the one you used in Lesson Four.) Jot down notes below. Include ideas about your audience's perspective and the response you want from your audience.

Topic:

My Audience:

Thesis Statement:

Support   1.

              2.

              3.

Opposing arguments that I'll need to refute:

Understanding the needs of your audience can help you build a strong, persuasive argument.

Focus on the Writer: Yoshiko Uchida

For a good part of her childhood, Yoshiko Uchida felt very much alone. She was born in Alameda, California, the daughter of two Japanese immigrants. Because her parents were Japanese and she was American, she sometimes felt like she didn't belong. To help fill the hours of the day, young Yoshiko turned to writing. She started out writing stories about Japanese and Japanese American children. When she was in her early twenties, she published many of her articles and folk tales about Japan. Later, she switched her focus and began writing about Japanese Americans and their experiences before, during, and after World War II.

In this unit you'll explore the works of Yoshiko Uchida. As you read, watch for questions, experiences, and feelings that remind you of yourself. How is your search for an identity similar to that of Uchida?

One A Writer's Heritage

Yoshiko Uchida often writes about people who are searching for an identity. "Who am I?" "Where do I belong?" "How do I fit in?" These are questions that many of Uchida's **characters** ask themselves over and over again. They are also questions that Uchida, as a young girl, asked herself.

For Yoshiko Uchida, the search for an identity began some two thousand miles from home. Determined to find her identity, Uchida traveled to Japan. While there, she spent most of her time learning everything she could about Japan—its customs, its history, and its people. During this period she found part of the answer to the question, "Who am I?"

Read this excerpt from the folk tale "The Princess of Light." As you read, underline words and phrases that show Uchida's respect for Japanese customs and history.

Response Notes

98

from **"The Princess of Light"** by Yoshiko Uchida

Once upon a time, there was an old man and an old woman who lived in a small village in Japan. Their little wooden house with the low thatched roof stood nestled against a hillside covered with trees. Each day the old man strapped his straw sandals on his feet and went out to the nearby bamboo thicket to cut down long, slender stalks of bamboo. When he brought them home, the old woman would help him cut and polish the smooth stalks. Then together they would make bamboo vases, baskets, flutes, and many beautiful ornaments which they could sell in the village.

They were good, kind, and honest people, and they worked very hard. They were happy, but they were lonesome, for they had no children. Both of them wanted a child more than anything else in the world.

"Oh, if only we had a little boy or a little girl, how happy we would be," sighed the old man.

"Yes, wouldn't that be wonderful!" answered the old woman. "I would rather have a child than all the riches on earth!"

And so each day they both knelt at the little shrine in the corner of their room, and prayed that some day they would be granted a child.

Now one day when the old man went out into the bamboo thicket, he saw one stalk which was shining so brightly it looked as though it were made of gold. He hurried toward it and looked at it closely, but he could not tell what made it shine.

"My, what a strange bamboo," said the old man to himself.

from **"The Princess of Light"** by Yoshiko Uchida

"Perhaps I'd better see what is inside." So he began to cut it down with the saw which he carried at his side. But suddenly he stopped, for he heard something very strange!

"What was that?" asked the old man. "It sounded like the crying of a baby!"

He straightened his back and looked all around, but he did not see anyone. All he could see were the stalks of bamboo swaying gently in the breeze.

He shook his head slowly and said, "My, I must be getting old to be hearing such strange sounds in a bamboo thicket."

He was turning again toward the shining bamboo when he heard the sound once more. He was sure this time that it was a baby crying, and the sound came right from inside the strange shiny stalk. Quickly he cut down the bamboo and looked inside the hollow of the stalk. There he saw a tiny baby girl! She looked up at the old man and smiled sweetly. And the old man was so surprised at this strange sight, he blinked hard and touched the little girl to see if she were real.

"My goodness! Good gracious! Oya-oya!" was all the old man could say. "This child must have been sent to us straight from heaven," he thought, as he picked her up very carefully. Then he quickly started homeward, for he could scarcely wait to show her to the old woman.

When the old woman saw the beautiful child, she threw up her hands in surprise. "God has been good to us!" she exclaimed. "We must take very good care of our little girl." Then she hurriedly set about spreading a quilt on the floor where she gently laid the new baby.

The next morning the old man was up bright and early. He whistled gaily as he walked toward the bamboo thicket. As he came closer to the spot where he had found the little baby the day before, he saw another bamboo which was shining brightly.

"I wonder if I will find another little baby," thought the old man, as he prepared to cut down the bamboo. He listened for any sound that might be the crying of a child, but he heard only the song of a sparrow as it flew into the thicket. This time, when he cut down the shiny bamboo stalk, a shower of gold coins fell to the ground. They glittered and sparkled, and seemed to tell the old man, "Take us home. We are yours!" The old man gathered up the coins and filled his moneybag. Then he hurried home once more, chuckling softly to himself to think how he would again surprise his wife.

When the old woman saw the coins, she said, "My, how lucky we are! Perhaps this is God's way of helping us provide for our little daughter. We must be grateful and take good care of her.

from **"The Princess of Light"** by Yoshiko Uchida

"Yes, yes, we shall always work hard and take good care of our child," said the old man.

From that day on, each time the old man went out to the bamboo thicket, he found one shiny golden stalk. When he cut it down, he always found the hollow filled with gold coins. Before long, the old man and woman became rich, but they continued to work hard.

The little baby of the bamboo was a wonderful child indeed. Each night she seemed to grow a whole year older, instead of just a day older. Each morning she surprised the old man and woman by being able to do or say something new.

"My, but she is a bright child," said the old woman.

"And see how much more beautiful she becomes each day," added the old man.

As she grew older, they discovered something even more wonderful about her. A beautiful, bright light seemed to glow all around her, just like the light which the old man had seen around the bamboo in which he found her. So the old man and woman decided to call their lovely daughter Kaguya Hime, which means Princess of Light. Their little home seemed to be filled with golden sunlight day and night, and they no longer had to use the lamps in the evening.

Kaguya Hime continued to grow in beauty each day, until soon the whole countryside had heard of her loveliness and of the radiant glow which she cast about her.

"She is like a lovely golden sunbeam," said some. "She is like sunshine on a rainbow," said others. "She is an angel from heaven," said still others; and everyone who knew her came to love her dearly.

●◆ Based on what you've read, what would you say is Uchida's attitude toward Japan?

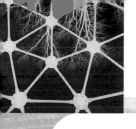

What connection can you make between "The Princess of Light" and the questions "Who am I?" and "Where do I belong?"

Imagine you are twenty-year-old Yoshiko Uchida, on an extended stay in Japan. Write a letter home to your parents. In your letter, explain your answers to the questions "Who am I?" and "Where do I belong?"

101

Authors, like many people, explore questions such as "Who am I?" and "Where do I belong?"

TWO A Writer's Identity

Because she was an American, Uchida wrote about Japan from an American perspective. For example, in *The Forever Christmas Tree*, Uchida tells the story of a Japanese boy who longs for a Christmas tree, even though his family does not celebrate Christmas:

> It was too cold to play outside, so Takashi sat where he could watch the road. He waited and waited for Kaya to come home from school. When at last he saw her, she was running, and Takashi knew she had something special to tell. As soon as she was in the house, the words came tumbling out.
>
> "Today we learned about Christmas!" she said, and the bright glow of her excitement quickly spilled out to fill Takashi too.
>
> Takashi did not know much about Christmas for no one celebrated it in Sugi Village. It was the New Year that mattered.

At times, Uchida felt torn between these two different cultures. In her **autobiography**, she describes how, as a child, she often felt as if she were being pulled in two completely different directions, never quite knowing who she was, or how she fit in. As you read this excerpt from Uchida's autobiography, underline or **highlight** information about the author's sense of identity.

102

Response notes

from *The Invisible Thread* by Yoshiko Uchida

I was born in California, recited the Pledge of Allegiance to the flag each morning at school, and loved my country as much as any other American—maybe even more.

Still, there was a large part of me that was Japanese simply because Mama and Papa had passed on to me so much of their own Japanese spirit and soul. Their own values of loyalty, honor, self-discipline, love, and respect for one's parents, teachers, and superiors were all very much a part of me.

There was also my name, which teachers couldn't seem to pronounce properly even when I shortened my first name to Yoshi. And there was my Japanese face, which closed more and more doors to me as I grew older.

How wonderful it would be, I used to think, if I had blond hair and blue eyes like Marian and Solveig. Or a name like Mary Anne Brown or Betty Johnson.

If only I didn't have to ask such questions as, "Can we come swim in your pool? We're Japanese." Or when we were looking for a house, "Will the neighbors object if we move in next door?" Or when I went for my first professional haircut, "Do you cut Japanese hair?"

Still, I didn't truly realize how different I was until the summer I was eleven. Although Papa usually went on business

from **The Invisible Thread** by Yoshiko Uchida

Response notes

trips alone, bringing back such gifts as silver pins for Mama or charm bracelets for Keiko and me, that summer he was able to take us along, thanks to a railroad pass.

We took the train, stopping at the Grand Canyon, Houston, New Orleans, Washington, D.C., New York, Boston, Niagara Falls, and on the way home, Chicago, to see the World's Fair.

Crossing the Mississippi River was a major event, as our train rolled onto a barge and sailed slowly over that grand body of water. We all got off the train for a closer look, and I was so impressed with the river's majesty, I felt impelled to make some kind of connection with it. Finally, I leaned over the barge rail and spit so a part of me would be in the river forever.

For my mother, the high point of the trip was a visit to the small village of Cornwall, Connecticut. There she had her first meeting with the two white American pen pals with whom she had corresponded since her days at Doshisha University. She also visited one of her former missionary teachers, Louise DeForest, who had retired there. And it was there I met a young girl my age, named Cathy Sellew. We became good friends, corresponded for many years, and met again as adults when I needed a home and a friend.

Everyone in the village greeted us warmly, and my father was asked to say a few words to the children of the Summer Vacation Church School—which he did with great relish.

Most of the villagers had never before met a Japanese American. One smiling woman shook my hand and said, "My, but you speak English so beautifully." She had meant to compliment me, but I was so astonished, I didn't know what to say. I realized she had seen only my outer self—my Japanese face—and addressed me as a foreigner. I knew then that I would always be different, even though I wanted so badly to be like my white American friends.

103

What are three things you learned about Uchida from reading this excerpt?

1.

2.

3.

➡️◆ As a child, Uchida felt as if she were three children rolled into one. Sometimes she was Japanese, sometimes she was American, and sometimes she was Japanese American. Review the notes you made while reading the excerpt from *The Invisible Thread*. Complete the diagram below by listing some of the ways Uchida felt as if she were three little girls in one.

YOSHIKO UCHIDA AS A CHILD

I am Japanese
American

I am Japanese

I am American

My name is Japanese.

104

When you read an autobiography, watch for the ways the author answers the questions "Who am I?" and "How do I fit in?" These questions will help you see how the author views himself or herself.

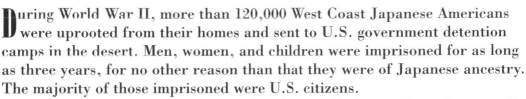

Three A Writer's Language

During World War II, more than 120,000 West Coast Japanese Americans were uprooted from their homes and sent to U.S. government detention camps in the desert. Men, women, and children were imprisoned for as long as three years, for no other reason than that they were of Japanese ancestry. The majority of those imprisoned were U.S. citizens.

In 1942, Yoshiko Uchida and her family were "relocated" to a horse stall at Tanforan racetrack in San Bruno, California. Later they were moved to Topaz, a Japanese American internment camp in Utah. The Uchida family spent many long, frightening months at Topaz.

For years after she was released, Yoshiko kept quiet about the alienation and rejection she felt as a result of her internment. In the early 1970s, however, she decided she would remain silent no longer. She wanted the world to know what her family and friends had experienced during the war. She wrote a series of books—fiction and nonfiction—that describe their experiences.

In her books about the detention camps, Uchida uses **sensory language** (words that can help you see, hear, touch, smell, or taste the thing described) as a way of giving readers a "you are there" feeling. As you read this excerpt from *Journey Home*, underline words and phrases that help you see, hear, smell, and even taste what it was like at the detention center in Topaz.

---

from *Journey Home* by Yoshiko Uchida

Response notes

I can't see, Yuki thought frantically. I can't breathe.

The screaming desert wind flung its white powdery sand in her face, stifling her and wrapping her up in a smothering cocoon of sand so fine it was like dust. It blinded her and choked her and made her gag as she opened her mouth to cry out.

The black tar-papered barracks on either side of the road had vanished behind the swirling dust, and Yuki was all alone in an eerie, unreal world where nothing existed except the shrieking wind and the great choking clouds of dust. Yuki stumbled on, doubled over, pushing hard against the wind, gasping as she felt the sting of sand and pebbles against her legs.

Suppose she never got back to her barrack? Suppose the wind simply picked her up and flung her out beyond the barbed wire fence into the desert? Suppose no one ever found her dried, wind-blown body out there in the sagebrush?

A cry of terror swelled up inside her. "Mama! Papa! Help me!"

●◆ What is your reaction to the passage you just read? Explain your feelings.

106

●◆Analyze the excerpt from *Journey Home*. Put any sensory words you find into the correct space on the web. Words that help you see something go in the "Sight Words" circle; words that help you know what something feels like go in the "Touch Words" circle, and so on.

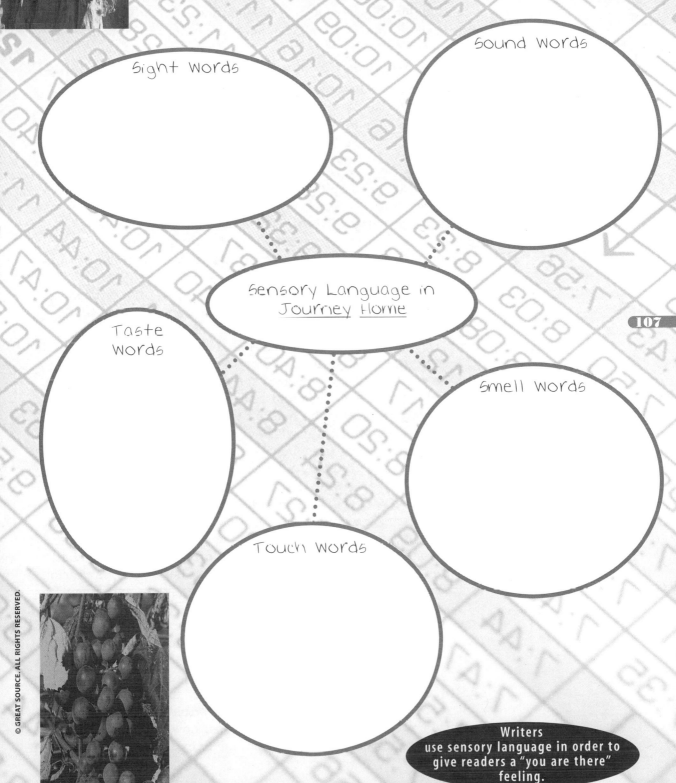

Sight Words

Sound Words

Sensory Language in Journey Home

Taste Words

Smell Words

Touch Words

107

Writers use sensory language in order to give readers a "you are there" feeling.

Four A Writer's Themes

Readers who are familiar with Uchida's work know that she explores two themes over and over again in her writing. The first theme—pride in one's ancestry—is a reflection of Uchida's own feelings about herself and her family. Her second major theme—courage during times of trouble—is especially apparent in her books about Japanese American internment camps.

As you read this excerpt from Uchida's memoir *Desert Exile,* watch for ideas that relate to these two themes. Does Uchida give the two themes equal weight in this selection? Make some notes in the margin. (*Issei* is a term for people born in Japan who live in America; *Nisei* are the American-born children of Issei parents.)

from *Desert Exile* by Yoshiko Uchida

Response notes

On my last day at school, the children of my class presented me with a clay bowl one of them had made, and they stood together, giggling and embarrassed, to sing one last song for me.

On our last Sunday, my sister and I went to say goodbye to all our friends, especially the older Issei who we knew would probably remain in camp until the end of the war.

It was hard for us to go, leaving behind our Issei parents in the desolation of that desert camp. And I imagine other Nisei felt as we did as they ventured forth into the outside world.

Because we Nisei were still relatively young at the time, it was largely the Issei who had led the way, guiding us through the devastation and trauma of our forced removal. When they were uprooted from their homes, many had just reached a point of financial security in their lives. During the war, however, they all suffered enormous losses, both tangible and intangible. The evacuation was the ultimate of the incalculable hardships and indignities they had borne over the years.

And yet most of our parents had continued to be steadfast and strong in spirit. Our mothers had made homes of the bleak barrack rooms, just as my own mother, in her gentle, nurturing way, had been a loving focal point for our family and friends.

Deprived of so much themselves, the Issei wanted the best for their Nisei children. Many had sacrificed to send their children to college, and they encouraged them now to leave camp to continue their education.

As my sister and I prepared for our departure, thoughts of gratitude toward our Issei parents still lay unspoken deep within us, and it was only in later years that we came to realize how much they had done for us; how much they had given us to enrich and strengthen our lives.

➥ Look over the notes you made about ancestry and courage while reading the selection. In the diagram below, list the ways that Uchida explores these themes in *Desert Exile*.

Taking Pride in One's Ancestry

She is respectful of the

sacrifices of the Issei.

Showing Courage in Times of Trouble

She bravely leaves her

parents behind.

109

●◆Now connect one of Uchida's themes to your own life. Write a journal entry describing a time you showed courage during a difficult period or a time you demonstrated pride in your heritage.

110

Understanding an author's themes can help you connect your reading to your own life.

Five
A Writer's Intent

Some authors write with the purpose of entertaining their readers. Others write in order to argue or persuade. Still others write so that they can teach readers about something that is important or meaningful. Many writers try to do a little bit of each.

What is Uchida's intent? Read this excerpt from an interview with Yoshiko Uchida. As you read her words, underline any clues about her purpose. Be sure to note your questions in the margin.

from an interview with Yoshiko Uchida

←Response notes →

I hope to give young Asians a sense of their own history. At the same time, I want to dispel the stereotypic image still held by many non-Asians about the Japanese Americans and write about them as real people. I hope to convey as well the strength of spirit and the sense of hope and purpose I have seen in many of the first generation Japanese Americans. Beyond that, I write to celebrate our common humanity, for I feel the basic elements of humanity are present in all our strivings.

111

●◆ Summarize in a few words Uchida's purpose for writing.

....

....

●◆ Think about this passage and other writings by Yoshiko Uchida. What have you learned from reading Uchida?

....

....

....

....

....

....

●❖ Reflect on what you know about Yoshiko Uchida—her life and her works. Use the graphic organizer below to make notes about her stories, themes, and messages.

Yoshiko Uchida: Writer, Storyteller, Teacher

What she writes about	In what book?	What lesson does she want to teach?

Some authors write with the intention of conveying to you, the reader, something they believe is important or meaningful.

The Reader's Response

When you pick up a book, magazine, or newspaper, you probably respond to the words on the page in at least three different ways. You respond on a *factual* level (you read and understand the facts the writer presents), on an *interpretive* level (you understand the meaning of those facts), and on an *evaluative* level (you liked this idea; you thought this story was strange, and so on).

Of course, reading is not just about the reader's response. Reading is learning and enjoying and wondering and analyzing and so much more. But your various responses can give you another set of tools to help you get the most out of what you read. In this unit, you'll discover just how useful these tools can be.

One
Factual Response

When you read a piece of writing, you respond to the **facts**—the things that are known to be true or to have really happened. When you respond factually, you ask and then answer five factual questions:

✔who?   ✔when?   ✔what?   ✔where?   ✔how?

As you read "Turkeys" by Bailey White, keep an eye out for important facts. Each time you see a word or sentence that relates to a who, what, where, when, and how, make a note in the margin.

Response Notes

114

"Turkeys" by Bailey White

Something about my mother attracts ornithologists. It all started years ago when a couple of them discovered she had a rare species of woodpecker coming to her bird feeder. They came in the house and sat around the window, exclaiming and taking pictures with big fancy cameras. But long after the red cockaded woodpeckers had gone to roost in their sticky little holes in the red hearts of our big old pine trees, and the chuck-will's-widows had started to sing their night chorus, the ornithologists were still there. There always seemed to be three or four of them wandering around our place, discussing the body fat of hummingbirds, telling cruel jokes about people who couldn't tell a pileated woodpecker from an ivory bill, and staying for supper.

In those days, during the 1950s, the big concern of ornithologists in our area was the wild turkey. They were rare, and the pure-strain wild turkeys had begun to interbreed with farmers' domestic stock. The species was being degraded. It was extinction by dilution, and to the ornithologists it was just as tragic as the more dramatic demise of the passenger pigeon or the Carolina parakeet.

One ornithologist had devised a formula to compute the ratio of domestic to pure-strain wild turkey in an individual bird by comparing the angle of flight at takeoff and the rate of acceleration. And in those sad days, the turkeys were flying low and slow.

It was during that time, the spring when I was six years old, that I caught the measles. I had a high fever, and my mother was worried about me. She kept the house quiet and dark and crept around silently, trying different methods of cooling me down.

Even the ornithologists stayed away—but not out of fear of the measles or respect for a household with sickness. The fact was, they had discovered a wild turkey nest. According to the

"Turkeys" by Bailey White

formula, the hen was pure-strain wild—not a taint of the
sluggish domestic bird in her blood—and the ornithologists
were camping in the woods, protecting her nest from predators
and taking pictures.

One night our phone rang. It was one of the ornithologists.
"Does your little girl still have measles?" he asked.

"Yes," said my mother. "She's very sick. Her temperature
is 102."

"I'll be right over," said the ornithologist.

In five minutes a whole carload of them arrived. They
marched solemnly into the house, carrying a cardboard box.
"A hundred two, did you say? Where is she?" they asked my
mother.

They crept into my room and set the box down on the bed.
I was barely conscious, and when I opened my eyes, their
worried faces hovering over me seemed to float out of the
darkness like giant, glowing eggs. They snatched the covers off
me and felt me all over. They consulted in whispers.

"Feels just right, I'd say."

"A hundred two—can't miss if we tuck them up close and
she lies still."

I closed my eyes then, and after a while the ornithologists
drifted away, their pale faces bobbing up and down on the
black wave of fever.

The next morning I was better. For the first time in days I
could think. The memory of the ornithologists with their
whispered voices and their bony, cool hands was like a dream
from another life. But when I pulled down the covers, there
staring up at me with googly eyes and wide mouths, were
sixteen fuzzy baby turkeys and the cracked chips and caps of
sixteen brown speckled eggs.

I was a sensible child. I gently stretched myself out. The
eggshells crackled, and the turkey babies fluttered and cheeped
and snuggled against me. I laid my aching head back on the
pillow and closed my eyes. "The ornithologists," I whispered.
"The ornithologists have been here."

It seems the turkey hen had been so disturbed by the
elaborate protective measures that had been undertaken on her
behalf that she had abandoned her nest on the night the eggs
were due to hatch. It was a cold night. The ornithologists, not
having an incubator to hand, used their heads and came up
with the next best thing.

The baby turkeys and I gained our strength together. When I
was finally able to get out of bed and feebly creep around the
house, the turkeys peeped and cheeped around my ankles,
scrambling to keep up with me and tripping over their own big

"Turkeys" by Bailey White

← Response notes

spraddle-toed feet. When I went outside for the first time, the turkeys tumbled after me down the steps and scratched around in the yard while I sat in the sun.

Finally, in late summer, the day came when they were ready to fly for the first time as adult birds. The ornithologists gathered. I ran down the hill, and the turkeys ran too. Then, one by one, they took off. They flew high and fast. The ornithologist made V's with their thumbs and forefingers, measuring angles. They consulted their stopwatches and paced off distances. They scribbled in their tiny notebooks. Finally they looked at each other. They sighed. They smiled. They jumped up and down and hugged each other. "One hundred percent pure wild turkey!" they said.

Nearly forty years have passed since then. In many ways the world is a worse place now. But there's a vaccine for measles. And the woods where I live are full of pure wild turkeys. I like to think they are all descendants of those sixteen birds I saved from the vigilance of the ornithologists.

👓 You are a reporter assigned to cover the wild turkey story for a magazine. Before you can write the article, you'll need to get your facts straight. Review the notes you made while reading "Turkeys." Then answer these questions:

116

- Who are the people involved?

- Where and when do the events take place?

- What happened and how did it happen?

●◆ Now write the opening paragraphs (called the *lead*) for your wild turkey article. Like any good reporter, you'll use your lead to cover who, what, where, when, and how. To add interest, you might want to include one or two "quotes" from your source.

117

Asking factual questions such as who, what, when, where, and how can help you understand and connect with what you read.

Two Interpretive Response

A second type of response is interpretive. *Interpreting* is like inferencing. When you interpret a selection, you make reasonable guesses about the selection's meaning. In other words, you ask the kinds of "why" questions that help you dig out the selection's meaning. When you read fiction, many of the interpretive questions you'll ask will be about the characters of the story. For example, you might ask why a character acts a particular way or says a particular thing or has a particular thought.

As you read the first part of "Charles," pay particular attention to Shirley Jackson's characters. Jot down any interpretive, or "why," questions in the response notes.

Response notes

"Charles" by Shirley Jackson

The day my son Laurie started kindergarten he renounced corduroy overalls with bibs and began wearing blue jeans with a belt; I watched him go off the first morning with the older girl next door, seeing clearly that an era of my life was ended, my sweet-voiced nursery-school tot replaced by a long-trousered, swaggering character who forgot to stop at the corner and wave good-bye to me.

He came home the same way, the front door slamming open, his cap on the floor, and the voice suddenly become raucous shouting, "Isn't anybody *here?*"

At lunch he spoke insolently to his father, spilled his baby sister's milk, and remarked that his teacher said we were not to take the name of the Lord in vain.

"How *was* school today?" I asked, elaborately casual.

"All right," he said.

"Did you learn anything?" his father asked.

Laurie regarded his father coldly. "I didn't learn nothing," he said.

"Anything," I said. "Didn't learn anything."

"The teacher spanked a boy, though," Laurie said, addressing his bread and butter. "For being fresh," he added, with his mouth full.

"What did he do?" I asked. "Who was it?"

Laurie thought. "It was Charles," he said. "He was fresh. The teacher spanked him and made him stand in a corner. He was awfully fresh."

"What did he do?" I asked again, but Laurie slid off his chair, took a cookie, and left, while his father was still saying, "See here, young man."

The next day Laurie remarked at lunch, as soon as he sat down, "Well, Charles was bad again today." He grinned enormously and said, "Today Charles hit the teacher."

"Charles" by Shirley Jackson

"Good heavens," I said, mindful of the Lord's name, "I suppose he got spanked again?"

"He sure did," Laurie said. "Look up," he said to his father.

"What?" his father said, looking up.

"Look down," Laurie said. "Look at my thumb. Gee, you're dumb." He began to laugh insanely.

"Why did Charles hit the teacher?" I asked quickly.

"Because she tried to make him color with red crayons," Laurie said. "Charles wanted to color with green crayons so he hit the teacher and she spanked him and said nobody play with Charles but everybody did."

The third day—it was Wednesday of the first week—Charles bounced a see-saw on to the head of a little girl and made her bleed, and the teacher made him stay inside all during recess. Thursday Charles had to stand in a corner during story-time because he kept pounding his feet on the floor. Friday Charles was deprived of blackboard privileges because he threw chalk.

On Saturday I remarked to my husband, "Do you think kindergarten is too unsettling for Laurie? All this toughness, and bad grammar, and this Charles boy sounds like such a bad influence."

"It'll be all right," my husband said reassuringly. "Bound to be people like Charles in the world. Might as well meet them now as later."

On Monday Laurie came home late, full of news. "Charles," he shouted as he came up the hill; I was waiting anxiously on the front steps. "Charles," Laurie yelled all the way up the hill, "Charles was bad again."

"Come right in," I said, as soon as he came close enough. "Lunch is waiting."

"You know what Charles did?" he demanded, following me through the door. "Charles yelled so in school they sent a boy in from first grade to tell the teacher she had to make Charles keep quiet, and so Charles had to stay after school. And so all the children stayed to watch him."

"What did he do?" I asked.

"He just sat there," Laurie said, climbing into his chair at the table. "Hi, Pop, y'old dust mop."

"Charles had to stay after school today," I told my husband. "Everyone stayed with him."

"What does this Charles look like?" my husband asked Laurie. "What's his other name?"

"He's bigger than me," Laurie said. "And he doesn't have any rubbers and he doesn't ever wear a jacket."

Monday night was the first Parent-Teachers meeting, and only the fact that the baby had a cold kept me from going; I wanted passionately to meet Charles's mother. On Tuesday

Laurie remarked suddenly, "Our teacher had a friend come to see her in school today."

"Charles's mother?" my husband and I asked simultaneously.

"Naaah," Laurie said scornfully. "It was a man who came and made us do exercises, we had to touch our toes. Look." He climbed down from his chair and squatted down and touched his toes. "Like this," he said. He got solemnly back into his chair and said, picking up his fork, "Charles didn't even *do* exercises."

"That's fine," I said heartily. "Didn't Charles want to do exercises?"

"Naaah," Laurie said. "Charles was so fresh to the teacher's friend he wasn't *let* do exercises."

"Fresh again?" I said.

"He kicked the teacher's friend," Laurie said. "The teacher's friend told Charles to touch his toes like I just did and Charles kicked him."

"What are they going to do about Charles, do you suppose?" Laurie's father asked him.

Laurie shrugged elaborately. "Throw him out of school, I guess," he said.

Wednesday and Thursday were routine; Charles yelled during story hour and hit a boy in the stomach and made him cry. On Friday Charles stayed after school again and so did all the other children.

With the third week of kindergarten Charles was an institution in our family; the baby was being a Charles when she cried all afternoon. Laurie did a Charles when he filled his wagon full of mud and pulled it through the kitchen; even my husband, when he caught his elbow in the telephone cord and pulled telephone, ashtray, and a bowl of flowers off the table, said, after the first minute, "Looks like Charles."

STOP

●◆Have you ever known anyone like Charles? Explain.

●◆ Write a "why" question about each of the characters in the space below. Then switch *Daybook*s with a partner and answer each other's questions as you imagine the characters would.

Laurie

Why . . . is Laurie so excited about the things Charles is doing at

school?

Answer:

Charles

Why . . .

Answer:

Laurie's Mom

Why . . .

Answer:

Laurie's Dad

Why . . .

Answer:

Discuss your answers. Were you and your partner able to interpret enough of the selection to answer the questions about each character? Why or why not?

To interpret a selection, begin by asking "why" questions about the characters.

Supporting Your Views

Good readers find support for the interpretations they come up with. When you support an interpretation, you find words, phrases, or sentences from the text to back up your interpretation. For example, let's say your interpretation is that Laurie's mother is obsessed with Charles. To support that interpretation, you might point out that she asks a lot of questions about him and allows Charles to become "an institution in our family."

Read the second half of "Charles." As you read, keep your character interpretations from Lesson Two in mind. Circle or underline any support you find for your interpretations.

← Response notes

"Charles" (continued) by Shirley Jackson

During the third and fourth weeks it looked like a reformation in Charles; Laurie reported grimly at lunch on Thursday of the third week, "Charles was so good today the teacher gave him an apple."

"What?" I said, and my husband added warily, "You mean Charles?"

"Charles," Laurie said. "He gave the crayons around and he picked up the books afterward and the teacher said he was her helper."

"What happened?" I asked incredulously.

"He was her helper, that's all," Laurie said, and shrugged.

"Can this be true, about Charles?" I asked my husband that night. "Can something like this happen?"

"Wait and see," my husband said cynically. "When you've got a Charles to deal with, this may mean he's only plotting."

He seemed to be wrong. For over a week Charles was the teacher's helper; each day he handed things out and he picked things up; no one had to stay after school.

"The P.T.A. meeting's next week again," I told my husband one evening. "I'm going to find Charles's mother there."

"Ask her what happened to Charles," my husband said. "I'd like to know."

"I'd like to know myself," I said.

On Friday of that week things were back to normal. "You know what Charles did today?" Laurie demanded at the lunch table, in a voice slightly awed. "He told a little girl to say a word and she said it and the teacher washed her mouth out with soap and Charles laughed."

"What word?" his father asked unwisely, and Laurie said, "I'll have to whisper it to you, it's so bad." He got down off his chair and went around to his father. His father bent his head down and Laurie whispered joyfully. His father's eyes widened.

"Charles" (continued) by Shirley Jackson

Response notes

"Did Charles tell the little girl to say *that?*" he asked respectfully.

"She said it *twice*," Laurie said. "Charles told her to say it *twice.*"

"What happened to Charles?" my husband asked.

"Nothing," Laurie said. "He was passing out the crayons."

Monday morning Charles abandoned the little girl and said the evil word himself three or four times, getting his mouth washed out with soap each time. He also threw chalk.

My husband came to the door with me that evening as I set out for the P.T.A. meeting. "Invite her over for a cup of tea after the meeting," he said. "I want to get a look at her."

"If only she's there," I said prayerfully.

"She'll be there," my husband said. "I don't see how they could hold a P.T.A. meeting without Charles's mother."

At the meeting I sat restlessly, scanning each comfortable matronly face, trying to determine which one hid the secret of Charles. None of them looked to me haggard enough. No one stood up in the meeting and apologized for the way her son had been acting. No one mentioned Charles.

After the meeting I identified and sought out Laurie's kindergarten teacher. She had a plate with a cup of tea and a piece of chocolate cake; I had a plate with a cup of tea and a piece of marshmallow cake. We maneuvered up to one another cautiously and smiled.

"I've been so anxious to meet you," I said. "I'm Laurie's mother."

"We're all so interested in Laurie," she said.

"Well he certainly likes kindergarten," I said. "He talks about it all the time."

"We had a little trouble adjusting, the first week or so," she said primly, "but now he's a fine little helper. With occasional lapses, of course."

"Laurie usually adjusts very quickly," I said. "I suppose this time it's Charles's influence."

"Charles?"

"Yes," I said, laughing, "You must have your hands full in that kindergarten, with Charles."

"Charles?" she said. "We don't have any Charles in the kindergarten."

●➡ **What do you think of the ending of Jackson's story?**

●◆ Review the notes you made about "Charles." Use the chart to give your interpretation of each character. Be sure to offer two to three pieces of support for your interpretation.

Laurie's mother is obsessed with Charles.

support

1. She can't stop asking questions about him.

2. She allows "Charles" to become an institution.

3.

Laurie's father is

support

1.

2.

3.

Laurie is

support

1.

2.

3.

Return to your partner's answers to your "why" questions in Lesson Two. Put a star next to the interpretations that you can support with evidence from the story.

A reader's interpretations need to be supported with evidence from the selection.

Four Evaluative Response

Readers also make evaluative responses to what they read. When you evaluate a selection, you might ask yourself questions such as these:

1. What do I think of this selection?
2. How does this selection relate to me?

When you ask "What do I think of the selection?" you make a judgment about the writing. You decide if you liked it, if you'd want to read it again, whether you'd recommend it to a friend.

Read "The King and the Shirt" by Leo Tolstoy. As you read, think about what you like and don't like about the fable. Jot down your thoughts in the response notes.

"The King and the Shirt" by Leo Tolstoy

← Response notes →

A king once fell ill.

"I will give half my kingdom to the man who can cure me," he said.

All his wise men gathered together to decide how the king could be cured. But no one knew. Only one of the wise men said what he thought would cure the king.

"If you can find a happy man, take his shirt, put it on the king—and the king will be cured."

The king sent his emissaries to search for a happy man. They traveled far and wide throughout his whole kingdom, but they could not find a happy man. There was no one who was completely satisfied: if a man was rich he was ailing; if he was healthy he was poor; if he was rich and healthy he had a bad wife; or if he had children they were bad—everyone had something to complain of.

Finally, late one night, the king's son was passing by a poor little hut and he heard someone say:

"Now, God be praised, I have finished my work, I have eaten my fill, and I can lie down and sleep! What more could I want?"

The king's son rejoiced and gave orders that the man's shirt be taken and carried to the king, and that the man be given as much money as he wanted.

The emissaries went in to take off the man's shirt, but the happy man was so poor that he had no shirt.

125

●◆ What did you think of Tolstoy's fable? Rate four aspects of the fable on a scale of one to five, five being the best. Circle the score that you think is most appropriate.

	(terrible)				(great)
The plot	1	2	3	4	5
The characters	1	2	3	4	5
The writing style	1	2	3	4	5
The moral lesson	1	2	3	4	5

●◆ Based on your ratings, would you recommend this tale to a friend? Why or why not?

126

When you make an evaluative response, you form an opinion about what you have read.

Five Connecting to Your Life

One kind of evaluative response involves forming an opinion about what you read. Another kind of evaluative response involves thinking about how the selection applies to your own life. You can ask, "In what ways does this story or character remind me of my own experiences or memories?" or "How would I react if I were confronted with the same problem or situation?" When you respond this way—when you compare your reading to your own life—you can better connect with the writing.

Of course, some pieces are easier to connect to than others. But you'd be surprised at the connections you can make once you think through various aspects of the piece. A checklist might help:

✔ Does a character remind you of yourself or someone you know?

✔ Is the **setting** familiar?

✔ Has something like this happened to you?

✔ Do you and the author share a similar **viewpoint**?

➡ Use the checklist to help you fill in the chart below.

Selection	Familiar Characters	Familiar Setting	Familiar Experience	Similar Viewpoint	Other
"Turkeys"	Her mom acted like mine.				
"Charles"					
"The King and the Shirt"					

127

➥Now use your chart to write a **journal** entry explaining which selection you connected to the most and why.

Relating
literature to your own life
can add meaning to the selection
and help you get the most out
of your reading.

Reading Nonfiction: Factual Stories

From newspapers to the Internet, from encyclopedias to instruction manuals, nonfiction surrounds you. **Expository nonfiction** explains facts and ideas. **Narrative nonfiction** tells true stories about people and places.

Nonfiction may seem to be the opposite of fiction. Yet nonfiction involves many of the same story techniques that bring fiction to life. And when you read nonfiction, some of the same active reading strategies you use with stories can increase your understanding and enjoyment. Personalizing, questioning, and making inferences all work as well with factual material as with fiction. In these pages, you'll find ways to use these and other strategies to get the most out of nonfiction writing.

One Big Picture, Small Parts

Good **nonfiction** writers supply plenty of **details** to illustrate their points. To make sense of expository writing, you need to sort the main ideas from the details. A **main idea** is a general statement, the "big idea" that the writer is trying to convey. **Details** are the "small parts"—specific names, dates, numbers, examples, anecdotes, quotes, and other bits and pieces used to create the overall picture.

Read below about the 1980 eruption of Mount St. Helens, a volcano in the state of Washington. Personalize your reading by circling details that interest you.

response notes

---

from *Volcano* by Patricia Lauber

For well over a hundred years the volcano slept. Each spring, as winter snows melted, its slopes seemed to come alive. Wildflowers bloomed in meadows. Bees gathered pollen and nectar. Birds fed, found mates, and built nests. Bears lumbered out of their dens. Herds of elk and deer feasted on fresh green shoots. Thousands of people came to hike, picnic, camp, fish, paint, bird-watch, or just enjoy the scenery. Logging crews felled tall trees and planted seedlings.

These people knew that Mount St. Helens was a volcano, but they did not fear it. To them it was simply a green and pleasant mountain, where forests of firs stretched up the slopes and streams ran clear and cold.

The mountain did not seem so trustworthy to geologists (scientists who study the earth). They knew that Mount St. Helens was dangerous. It was a young volcano and one of the most active in the Cascade Range. In 1975, two geologists finished a study of the volcano's past eruptions. They predicted that Mount St. Helens would erupt again within 100 years, perhaps before the year 2000.

The geologists were right. With the earthquake of March 20, 1980, Mount St. Helens woke from a sleep of 123 years. Magma had forced its way into the mountain, tearing apart solid rock. The snapping of that rock set off the shock waves that shook St. Helens. That quake was followed by many others. Most of them were smaller, but they came so fast and so often that it was hard to tell when one quake ended and another began.

On March 27, people near Mount St. Helens heard a tremendous explosion. The volcano began to blow out steam and ash that stained its snow-white peak. Small explosions went on into late April, stopped, started again on May 7, and stopped on May 14.

from *Volcano* by Patricia Lauber

The explosions of late March opened up two new craters at the top of the mountain. One formed inside the old crater. The other formed nearby. The two new craters grew bigger. Soon they joined, forming one large crater that continued to grow during the next few weeks. Meanwhile, the north face of the mountaintop was swelling and cracking. The swelling formed a bulge that grew outward at a rate of five to six feet a day.

Geologists were hard at work on the waking volcano. They took samples of ash and gases, hoping to find clues to what was happening inside. They placed instruments on the mountain to record earthquakes and the tilting of ground. They kept measuring the bulge. A sudden change in its rate of growth might be a sign that the volcano was about to erupt. But the bulge grew steadily, and the ash and gases yielded no clues.

By mid-May, the bulge was huge. Half a mile wide and more than a mile long, it had swelled out 300 feet.

On Sunday morning, May 18, the sun inched up behind the Cascades, turning the sky pink. By 8:00 A.M. the sun was above the mountains, the sky blue, the air cool. There was not one hint of what was to come.

At 8:32, Mount St. Helens erupted. Billowing clouds of smoke, steam, and ash hid the mountain from view and darkened the sky for miles.

The eruption went on until evening. By its end a fan-shaped area of destruction stretched out to the north, covering some 230 square miles. Within that area 57 people and countless plants and animals had died.

●◆ **What questions about the eruption remain in your mind?**

●◆ Look again at the selection. What general idea about people's impressions of Mount St. Helens do these paragraphs convey to you? What details illustrate that idea?

Detail

Detail

Detail

Main Idea
Most people saw
the mountain as

....

....

but geologists saw it as

....

....

....

Detail

Detail

Detail

132

Sorting out main ideas and details can help you understand expository writing.

Two Broad Statements

One way to connect with nonfiction material is to use it to make your own generalizations. Making a **generalization** means:

1. taking specific information that you read, and

2. applying it to gain a broader, general insight.

Here's how:

Specifics:

Explosions came from St. Helens for two months before it erupted.

One side of St. Helens bulged out over 300 feet in the months before it erupted.

Dozens of earthquakes shook St. Helens before it erupted.

St. Helens began releasing steam and ash months before it erupted.

Generalization:

Volcanoes may give warning signs for months before erupting.

Notice that each specific statement is about one volcano, but the generalization jumps to a broader statement about all volcanoes.

In the next excerpt from *Volcano*, Lauber explains the "inside story" that geologists discovered about the eruption of Mount St. Helens. As you read, watch for specifics that you might use to make your own generalizations. **133** Mark these specifics with an S in your response notes.

from *Volcano* by Patricia Lauber

Response notes

The May 18 eruption began with an earthquake that triggered an avalanche. At 8:32 A.M., instruments that were miles away registered a strong earthquake. The pilot and passengers of a small plane saw the north side of the mountain rippling and churning. Shaken by the quake, the bulge was tearing loose. It began to slide, in a huge avalanche that carried along rock ripped from deep inside Mount St. Helens.

The avalanche tore open the mountain. A scalding blast shot sideways out of the opening. It was a blast of steam, from water heated by rising magma.

Normally water cannot be heated beyond its boiling point, which is 212 degrees Fahrenheit at sea level. At boiling point, water turns to a gas, which we call steam. But if water is kept under pressure, it can be heated far beyond its boiling point and still stay liquid. (That is how a pressure cooker works.) If the pressure is removed, this superheated water suddenly turns, or flashes, to steam. As steam it takes up much more room—it expands. The sudden change to steam can cause an explosion.

← Response notes

Before the eruption Mount St. Helens was like a giant pressure cooker. The rock inside it held superheated water. The water stayed liquid because it was under great pressure, sealed in the mountain. When the mountain was torn open, the pressure was suddenly relieved. The superheated water flashed to steam. Expanding violently, it shattered rock inside the mountain and exploded out the opening, traveling at speeds of up to 200 miles an hour.

The blast flattened whole forests of 180-foot-high firs. It snapped off or uprooted the trees, scattering the trunks as if they were straws. At first, this damage was puzzling. A wind of 200 miles an hour is not strong enough to level forests of giant trees. The explanation, geologists later discovered, was that the wind carried rocks ranging in size from grains of sand to blocks as big as cars. As the blast roared out of the volcano, it swept up and carried along the rock it had shattered.

The result was what one geologist described as "a stone wind." It was a wind of steam and rocks, traveling at high speed. The rocks gave the blast its great force. Before it, trees snapped and fell. Their stumps looked as if they had been sandblasted. The wind of stone rushed on. It stripped bark and branches from trees and uprooted them, leveling 150 square miles of countryside. At the edge of this area other trees were left standing, but the heat of the blast scorched and killed them.

The stone wind was traveling so fast that it overtook and passed the avalanche. On its path was Spirit Lake, one of the most beautiful lakes in the Cascades. The blast stripped the trees from the slopes surrounding the lake and moved on.

Meanwhile the avalanche had hit a ridge and split. One part of it poured into Spirit Lake, adding a 180-foot layer of rock and dirt to the bottom of the lake. The slide of avalanche into the lake forced the water out. The water sloshed up the slopes, then fell back into the lake. With it came thousands of trees felled by the blast.

The main part of the avalanche swept down the valley of the North Fork of the Toutle River. There, in the valley, most of the avalanche slowed and stopped. It covered 24 square miles and averaged 150 feet thick.

The blast itself continued for 10 to 15 minutes, then stopped. Minutes later, Mount St. Helens began to erupt upward. A dark column of ash and ground-up rock rose miles into the sky. Winds blew the ash eastward. Lightning flashed in the ash cloud and started forest fires. In Yakima, Washington, some 80 miles away, the sky turned so dark that street lights went on at noon. Ash fell like snow that would not melt. This eruption continued for nine hours.

●◆ Which details of the eruption or its aftermath can you picture most clearly?

●◆ Consider the work done by the scientists studying the eruption of Mount St. Helens. Scan both excerpts again to review information about their work. What generalization can you make about the efforts of scientists? (A generalization that is too broad can be inaccurate. To keep your generalizations accurate, avoid words such as *all*, *always*, *none*, or *never*. Instead, use qualifiers—words such as *most*, *usually*, *few*, or *seldom*.)

135

●◆ List three specific details that support your generalization.

1.

2.

3.

When you make generalizations based on your reading, you discover your own ways to apply the author's ideas.

The best readers question as they read. When you read **nonfiction**, ask yourself questions starting with "why" and "how."

• Why did this occur?

• How does this affect things?

Questions like these focus your thinking on **causes and effects**, sharpening your understanding. As you ask and answer these questions, you realize that one cause can have many effects, and one effect can have many causes.

As you read the selection below, jot "why" and "how" questions in the response notes.

← Response notes

"Mr. Misenheimer's Garden" from *On the Road with Charles Kuralt* by Charles Kuralt

We've been wandering the back roads since 1967, and we've been to a few places we'll never forget. One of them was on Route 10, Surry County, Virginia. We rolled in here on a day in the spring of 1972 thinking this was another of those little roadside rest stops. But there were flowers on the picnic tables. That was the first surprise.

And beyond the tables, we found a paradise, a beautiful garden of thirteen acres, bright with azaleas, thousands of them, and bordered by dogwoods in bloom, and laced by a mile of paths in the shade of tall pines. In all our travels, it was the loveliest garden I'd ever seen. It made me wonder how large a battalion of state-employed gardeners it took to keep the place up. The answer was it took one old man, and he was nobody's employee. Walter Misenheimer, a retired nurseryman, created all this in the woods next to his house, created it alone after he retired at the age of seventy. He was eighty-three when I met him and was spending every day tending his garden for the pleasure of strangers who happened to stop.

Walter Misenheimer: I like people, and this is my way of following out some of the teachings of my parents. When I was a youngster, one of the things they said was, "If you don't try to make the world just a little bit nicer when you leave here, what is the reason for man's existence in the first place?" I have tried to give it to the state. The Parks Department says it is too small for them. The Highway Department says it is too big for them.

Kuralt: What's going to happen to this place after you're gone?

Misenheimer: Well, I imagine that within a very few years, this will be undergrowth, or nature will take it over again.

Kuralt: You mean, it's not going to survive?

Misenheimer: I doubt it.

"Mr. Misenheimer's Garden" from *On the Road with Charles Kuralt* by Charles Kuralt

Response notes

Kuralt: That's a terribly discouraging thing, isn't it?
Misenheimer: Well, that's the way I see it now.

We watched for a while as people enjoyed the beauty of Walter Misenheimer's garden. And we left, and a few years later somebody sent me a clipping from the Surry County paper. It said Walter Misenheimer had died. I wondered what would happen to his garden. I wondered whether the Virginia sun still lights the branches of the dogwood, which he planted there.

Well, it does. Some stories have happy endings. Walter Misenheimer's garden does survive, and so does his spirit, in Haeja Namkoong. It seems that she stopped by the garden just a few months after we did, eleven years ago.

Haeja Namkoong: We slowed down and saw a sign and picnic tables and a lot of flowers blooming. We came to the picnic table, found a water spigot, helped ourselves, and we were sort of curious as to what this place was all about. Finally, we saw the old man sort of wobbling around and coming 'cross the lawn, saying "Hello," and just waving to us to stop. I guess he was afraid we were going to leave.

To please the old man, and herself, Haeja Namkoong stayed the afternoon with him, walking in his garden. It made her remember, she says, something she wanted once.

Haeja: I grew up in a large city in Korea, and I have never really seen rice grow. I always dreamed about living in the country, about a small, little cabin in the wilderness, with lots of flowers. That's what I dreamed about, but I guess that was just childhood dreams.

When the sun went down that day, the young woman said good-bye to the old man and headed home to Boston, but the roadside Eden called her back. That is, Walter Misenheimer did. He phoned her, long distance, and asked her to come for a little while and help in the garden.

Haeja: He was sort of pleading with me, "Please come down. Just help me for a couple of weeks."

A couple of weeks only, and then a few more, and then it was Christmas. Haeja Namkoong was twenty-six. She had no family. Neither did Walter Misenheimer and his wife.

Haeja: From wildflowers to man-grown shrubberies, he taught me. I was interested in learning the whole thing. I was out here almost every day with him.

They became as father and daughter working in the garden,

137

←Response notes

and in time Haeja Namkoong was married in the garden.

Haeja: He was very proud to give me away. I guess he never thought, since he didn't have any children of his own, he would give someone away.

Brown earth was coaxed by the gentle old man into green growth and flowering red and pink and white. The earth rewards every loving attention it is paid. People repay such love, too, in memory.

Haeja: I was very, very close to my mother. But other than my mother, I can't remember anyone that loved me so much and cared for me so much as Mr. Misenheimer.

The garden is still here. Walter Misenheimer died in 1979 and left it to Haeja Namkoong. She pays a caretaker, Ed Trible, to help keep it beautiful for anyone who passes by. Haeja and her husband and their children live in Richmond now, but they return on weekends to work in the garden.

Haeja: So, knowing how much the garden meant to him, I want to keep it up and carry on.

Walter Misenheimer told me that he expected when he was gone the garden would soon be overgrown. He might have known better. His garden shows that something grows from seeds and cultivation. And if what you plant is love and kindness, something grows from that, too.

Haeja: Look at this purple one.
Child: I like the red.
Haeja: Aren't they pretty?

138

●◆Describe someone you know, or know of, who reminds you in some way of Mr. Misenheimer.

....

....

....

....

....

●◆Complete each sentence with a cause or an effect. (Remember: There's more than one "right" answer, since every event has multiple causes and effects.) Then add one more cause-and-effect sentence of your own. It can be about any part of the selection.

Effects		Causes
Mr. Misenheimer started his garden	because	
Haeja worked with Mr. Misenheimer	because	
	because	Haeja and the Misenheimers had no other family.
	because	Haeja honors the memory of Mr. Misenheimer.
	because	

Considering causes and effects helps you connect ideas as you read.

Four If...Then...

A conclusion is a kind of **inference**, or reasonable guess. When you draw a conclusion, you take a general idea or statement from your reading and apply it to a more specific situation. Think of a conclusion as an "if . . . then . . ." statement: *If* the general information holds true, *then* the specific conclusion should also hold true. You can use two steps to draw conclusions from a general statement.

General statement: Most mammals can swim.

1. Make it specific: A tiger is a mammal.

2. Draw your conclusion: A tiger can probably swim.

The general information applies to all kinds of mammals, while the conclusion zooms in on one specific kind of mammal.

➥ Reread "Mr. Misenheimer's Garden." See what leads up to the following statements by Charles Kuralt. Then use the two steps to draw your own conclusions about what Kuralt means when he says:

"His garden shows that something grows from seeds and cultivation. And if what you plant is love and kindness, something grows from that, too."

General statement: "...if what you plant is love and kindness, something grows from that, too."

1. Make it specific: A person might "plant love and kindness" by

....

....

....

2. Draw your conclusion: One result that might "grow" from those actions
could be

....

....

140

➥ Use the two steps to draw a conclusion based on another general statement from "Mr. Misenheimer's Garden."

General statement: "The earth rewards every loving attention it is paid."

1. Make it specific:

....

....

....

....

....

141

2. Draw your conclusion:

....

....

....

....

....

....

....

....

Drawing conclusions helps you think more deeply about the meaning of what you read.

Five

Nonfiction writers often use a compare-and-contrast pattern to organize information. Recognizing this pattern can make it easier for you to understand what you read. One way to spot the pattern is to look for similarities and differences in people or ideas being described.

In "A Sea Worry," the **narrator** is a teacher living in Hawaii. Decide how her views are like—and unlike—the views of the young people she describes.

← Response notes

from "A Sea Worry" by Maxine Hong Kingston

This summer my son body-surfs. He says it's his "job" and rises each morning at 5:30 to catch the bus to Sandy Beach. I hope that by September he will have had enough of the ocean. Tall waves throw surfers against the shallow bottom. Undertows have snatched them away. Sharks prowl Sandy's. Joseph told me that once he got out of the water because he saw an enormous shark. "Did you tell the lifeguard?" I asked. "No." "Why not?" "I didn't want to spoil the surfing." The ocean pulls at the boys, who turn into surfing addicts. At sunset you can see the surfers waiting for the last golden wave.

"Why do you go surfing so often?" I ask my students.

"It feels so good," they say. "Inside the tube, I can't describe it. There are no words for it."

"You can describe it," I scold, and I am very angry. "Everything can be described. Find the words for it, you lazy boy. Why don't you go home and read?" I am afraid that the boys give themselves up to the ocean's mindlessness.

When the waves are up, surfers all over Hawaii don't do their homework. They cut school. They know how the surf is breaking at any moment because every fifteen minutes the reports come over the radio; in fact, one of my former students is the surf reporter.

Some boys leave for mainland colleges, and write their parents heartrending letters. They beg to come home for Thanksgiving. "If I can just touch the ocean," they write from Missouri and Kansas, "I'll last for the rest of the semester." Some come home for Christmas and don't go back.

Even when the assignment is about something else, the students write about surfing. They try to describe what it is to be inside the wave as it curls over them, making a tube or "chamber" or "green room" or "pipeline" or "time warp." They write about the silence, the peace, "no hassles," the feeling of being reborn as they shoot out the end. They've written about the perfect wave. Their writing is full of clichés. "The endless summer," they say. "Unreal."

Surfing is like a religion. Among the martyrs are George Helm, Kimo Mitchell, and Eddie Aikau. Helm and Mitchell were

from **"A Sea Worry"** by Maxine Hong Kingston

Response notes

lost at sea riding their surfboards from Kaho'olawe, where they had gone to protest the Navy's bombing of that island. Eddie Aikau was a champion surfer and lifeguard. A storm had capsized the *Hokule'a*, the ship that traced the route that the Polynesian ancestors sailed from Tahiti, and Eddie Aikau had set out on his board to get help.

Since the ocean captivates our son, we decided to go with him to Sandy's.

We got up before dawn, picked up his friend, Marty, and drove out of Honolulu. Almost all the traffic was going in the opposite direction, the freeway coned to make more lanes into the city. We came to a place where raw mountains rose on our left and the sea fell on our right, smashing against the cliffs. The strip of cliff pulverized into sand is Sandy's. "Dangerous Current Exist," said the ungrammatical sign.

Earll and I sat on the shore with our blankets and thermos of coffee. Joseph and Marty put on their fins and stood at the edge of the sea for a moment, touching the water with their fingers and crossing their hearts before going in. There were fifteen boys out there, all about the same age, fourteen to twenty, all with the same kind of lean v-shaped build, most of them with black hair that made their wet heads look like sea lions. It was hard to tell whether our kid was one of those who popped up after a big wave. A few had surfboards, which are against the rules at a body-surfing beach, but the lifeguard wasn't on duty that day.

As they watched for the next wave, the boys turned toward the ocean. They gazed slightly upward; I thought of altar boys before a great god. When a good wave arrived, they turned, faced shore, and came shooting in, some taking the wave to the right and some to the left, their bodies fish-like, one arm out in front, the hand and fingers pointed before them, like a swordfish's beak. A few held credit card trays, and some slid in on trays from MacDonald's.

"This is no country for middle-aged women," I said. We had on bathing suits underneath our clothes in case we felt moved to participate. There were no older men either.

Even from the shore, we could see inside the tubes. Sometimes, when they came at an angle, we saw into them a long way. When the wave dug into the sand, it formed a brown tube or a golden one. The magic ones, though, were made out of just water, green and turquoise rooms, translucent walls and ceilings. I saw one that was powder-blue, perfect, thin; the sun filled it with sky blue and white light. The best thing, the kids say, is when you are in the middle of the tube, and there is water all around you but you're dry.

●◆Kingston and the surfers view surfing very differently. Still, they have some responses in common. Reread the selection, looking for direct statements about surfing. Make **inferences** about views that are suggested but not directly stated. Then fill in the Venn diagram below.

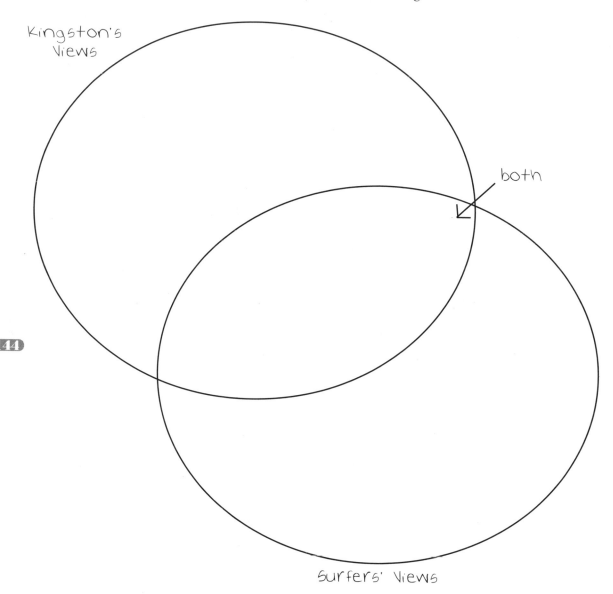

Kingston's Views

both

Surfers' Views

●◆Using your Venn diagram, draw one conclusion about Kingston's and the surfers' views on surfing. Write your conclusion below.

....

....

....

Comparing and contrasting ideas helps you understand and analyze what you read.

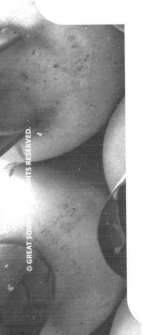

Conflict: The Driving Force

The driving force behind most stories is **conflict**: a clash of opposing energies. Almost all story plots feature characters trying to resolve conflicts. If you can identify the conflicts in a story, you will find it easier to understand the plot. You also gain insights into why the characters behave as they do. As conflicts intensify, you may feel suspense: a buildup of excitement and curiosity about the outcome.

In this unit, you'll explore five types of conflict:

- character vs. character
- character vs. self
- character vs. destiny
- character vs. society
- character vs. nature

One
Head to Head

In literature as in sports, two characters sometimes come into direct conflict. The **conflict** may be a physical competition, even a fight; or it may be a battle of words, wits, wills, or emotions. At the end of the story, one character may emerge victorious, or both characters may change a bit and learn to live with their differences.

As you read the selection below, ask yourself exactly what the conflict is. Try to see both characters' viewpoints.

"Shells" by Cynthia Rylant

response notes

"You *hate* living here."

Michael looked at the woman speaking to him.

"No, Aunt Esther. I don't." He said it dully, sliding his milk glass back and forth on the table. "I don't hate it here."

Esther removed the last pan from the dishwasher and hung it above the oven.

"You hate it here," she said, "and you hate me."

"I don't!" Michael yelled. "It's not *you!*"

The woman turned to face him in the kitchen.

"Don't yell at me!" she yelled. "I'll not have it in my home. I can't make you happy, Michael. You just refuse to be happy here. And you punish me every day for it."

"*Punish* you?" Michael gawked at her. "I don't punish you! I don't care about you! I don't care what you eat or how you dress or where you go or what you think. Can't you just leave me alone?"

He slammed down the glass, scraped his chair back from the table and ran out the door.

"Michael!" yelled Esther.

They had been living together, the two of them, for six months. Michael's parents had died and only Esther could take him in—or, only she had offered to. Michael's other relatives could not imagine dealing with a fourteen-year-old boy. They wanted peaceful lives.

Esther lived in a condominium in a wealthy section of Detroit. Most of the area's residents were older (like her) and afraid of the world they lived in (like her). They stayed indoors much of the time. They trusted few people.

Esther liked living alone. She had never married or had children. She had never lived anywhere but Detroit. She liked her condominium.

But she was fiercely loyal to her family, and when her only sister had died, Esther insisted she be allowed to care for Michael. And Michael, afraid of going anywhere else, had accepted.

146

"Shells" by Cynthia Rylant

Oh, he was lonely. Even six months after their deaths, he still expected to see his parents—sitting on the couch as he walked into Esther's living room, waiting for the bathroom as he came out of the shower, coming in the door late at night. He still smelled his father's Old Spice somewhere, his mother's talc.

Sometimes he was so sure one of them was *somewhere* around him that he thought maybe he was going crazy. His heart hurt him. He wondered if he would ever get better.

And though he denied it, he did hate Esther. She was so different from his mother and father. Prejudiced—she admired only those who were white and Presbyterian. Selfish—she wouldn't allow him to use her phone. Complaining—she always had a headache or a backache or a stomachache.

He didn't want to, but he hated her. And he didn't know what to do except lie about it.

Michael hadn't made any friends at his new school, and his teachers barely noticed him. He came home alone every day and usually found Esther on the phone. She kept in close touch with several other women in nearby condominiums.

Esther told her friends she didn't understand Michael. She said she knew he must grieve for his parents, but why punish her? She said she thought she might send him away if he couldn't be nicer. She said she didn't deserve this.

But when Michael came in the door, she always quickly changed the subject.

One day after school Michael came home with a hermit crab. He had gone into a pet store, looking for some small, living thing, and hermit crabs were selling for just a few dollars. He'd bought one, and a bowl.

Esther, for a change, was not on the phone when he arrived home. She was having tea and a crescent roll and seemed cheerful. Michael wanted badly to show someone what he had bought. So he showed her.

Esther surprised him. She picked up the shell and poked the long, shiny nail of her little finger at the crab's claws.

"Where is he?" she asked.

Michael showed her the crab's eyes peering through the small opening of the shell.

"Well, for heaven's sake, come out of there!" she said to the crab, and she turned the shell upside down and shook it.

"Aunt Esther!" Michael grabbed for the shell.

"All right, all right." She turned it right side up. "Well," she said, "what does he do?"

Michael grinned and shrugged his shoulders.

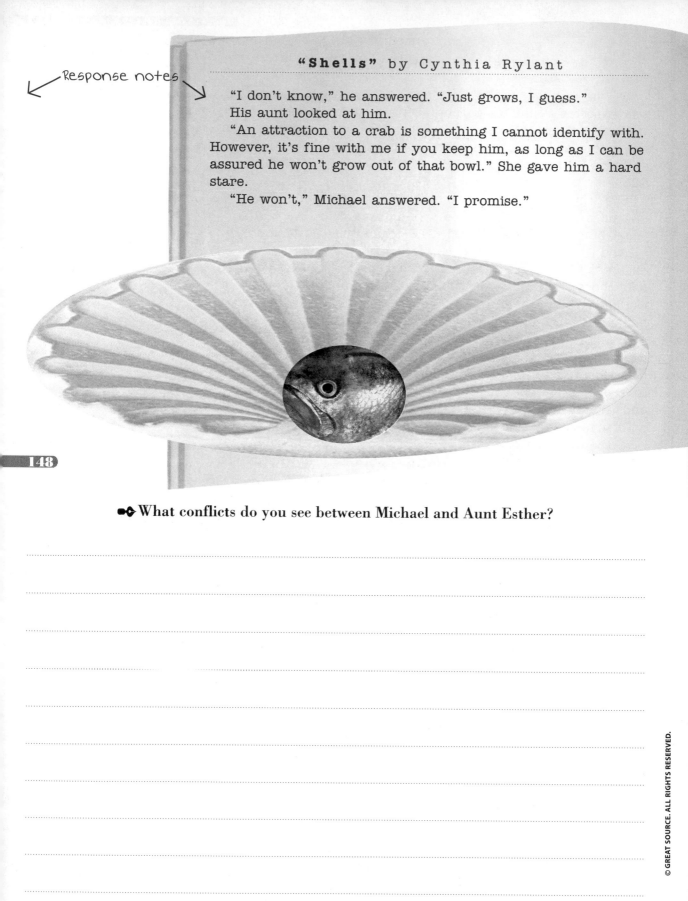

"Shells" by Cynthia Rylant

"I don't know," he answered. "Just grows, I guess."
His aunt looked at him.

"An attraction to a crab is something I cannot identify with. However, it's fine with me if you keep him, as long as I can be assured he won't grow out of that bowl." She gave him a hard stare.

"He won't," Michael answered. "I promise."

●◆ **What conflicts do you see between Michael and Aunt Esther?**

◗ Try to examine the conflict in the story from each character's perspective. In the left column, describe how Michael feels about his aunt and their living situation. In the right column, describe Aunt Esther's view of the situation and her nephew.

Michael	Aunt Esther

◗ Which character do you sympathize with most? Explain your response.

◗ How do you think that Michael and Aunt Esther might resolve their conflicts? Make a prediction.

Good readers increase their understanding by thinking about conflicts between characters.

Two

Me, Myself, and I

An internal conflict involves a character struggling with his or her own thoughts or emotions. Real-life people face internal conflicts, as do story characters. Internal conflicts make story characters seem more realistic. A character may be trying to make a decision, to understand an issue, to overcome a problem, or simply to grow as a human being. By watching characters struggle to resolve inner conflicts, we can gain insight into the characters and into real-life people as well.

Read the rest of "Shells." This time, watch for Michael's inner conflicts.

Response notes →

"Shells" (continued) by Cynthia Rylant

The hermit crab moved into the condominium. Michael named him Sluggo and kept the bowl beside his bed. Michael had to watch the bowl for very long periods of time to catch Sluggo with his head poking out of his shell, moving around. Bedtime seemed to be Sluggo's liveliest part of the day, and Michael found it easy to lie and watch the busy crab as sleep slowly came on.

One day Michael arrived home to find Esther sitting on the edge of his bed, looking at the bowl. Esther usually did not intrude in Michael's room, and seeing her there disturbed him. But he stood at the doorway and said nothing.

Esther seemed perfectly comfortable, although she looked over at him with a frown on her face.

"I think he needs a companion," she said.

"What?" Michael's eyebrows went up as his jaw dropped down.

Esther sniffed.

"I think Sluggo needs a girl friend." She stood up. "Where is that pet store?"

Michael took her. In the store was a huge tank full of hermit crabs.

"Oh my!" Esther grabbed the rim of the tank and craned her neck over the side. "Look at them!"

Michael was looking more at his Aunt Esther than at the crabs. He couldn't believe it.

"Oh, look at those shells. You say they grow out of them?" We must stock up with several sizes. See the pink in that one? Michael, look! He's got his little head out!"

Esther was so dramatic—leaning into the tank, her bangle bracelets clanking, earrings swinging, red pumps clicking on the linoleum—that she attracted the attention of everyone in

150

"Shells" (continued) by Cynthia Rylant

Response notes

the store. Michael pretended not to know her well.

He and Esther returned to the condominium with a thirty-gallon tank and twenty hermit crabs.

Michael figured he'd have a heart attack before he got the heavy tank into their living room. He figured he'd die and Aunt Esther would inherit twenty-one crabs and funeral expenses.

But he made it. Esther carried the box of crabs.

"Won't Sluggo be surprised?" she asked happily. "Oh, I do hope we'll be able to tell him apart from the rest. He's their founding father!"

Michael, in a stupor over his Aunt Esther and the phenomenon of twenty-one hermit crabs, wiped out the tank, arranged it with gravel and sticks (as well as the plastic scuba diver Aunt Esther insisted on buying) and assisted her in loading it up, one by one, with the new residents. The crabs were as overwhelmed as Michael. Not one showed its face.

Before moving Sluggo from his bowl, Aunt Esther marked his shell with some red fingernail polish so she could distinguish him from the rest. Then she flopped down on the couch beside Michael.

"Oh, what would your mother *think*, Michael, if she could see this mess we've gotten ourselves into!"

She looked at Michael with a broad smile, but it quickly disappeared. The boy's eyes were full of pain.

"Oh, my," she whispered. "I'm sorry."

Michael turned his head away.

Aunt Esther, who had not embraced anyone in years, gently put her arm about his shoulders.

"I am so sorry, Michael. Oh, you must hate me."

Michael sensed a familiar smell then. His mother's talc.

He looked at his aunt.

"No, Aunt Esther." He shook his head solemnly. "I don't hate you."

Esther's mouth trembled and her bangles clanked as she patted his arm. She took a deep, strong breath.

"Well, let's look in on our friend Sluggo," she said.

They leaned their heads over the tank and found him. The crab, finished with the old home that no longer fit, was coming out of his shell.

151

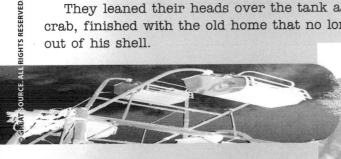

●◆ What do you think of the way the story turns out?

....

....

....

....

●◆ Michael is a little like Sluggo. Both wear a protective shell, and neither likes being poked at or shaken up. Read the whole story once more, underlining parts that show Michael's conflicting emotions. Then, in the blanks below, write down the internal conflicts that you see in Michael. (One is done for you.) Add more ideas of your own.

wants to be left alone   vs.   feels lonely

wants not to hate Aunt Esther   vs.

                                                         vs.

                                                         vs.

●◆ By the end of the story, which inner conflicts do you think Michael has resolved? Explain in a paragraph.

....

....

....

....

....

....

....

....

....

As you read, watch for internal conflicts that reveal opposing thoughts or feelings within a character.

Three
The Shape of Destiny

In a Norse myth, the god Thor agrees to wrestle a frail old woman. To his astonishment, she wins. Only later does he learn that the woman is Fate itself—which not even a god can overcome. Like Thor, some story characters struggle against fate—a fixed, unchangeable destiny. Whether or not we admire their efforts, we usually find the conflict compelling. After all, what human being doesn't want to be in charge of his or her own destiny?

As you read the traditional tale below, decide who is trying to change his destiny.

"Appointment in Baghdad" retold by Edith Wharton

Response notes

One morning the Sultan was resting in his palace in Damascus. Suddenly the door flew open, and in rushed a young man, out of breath and wild with excitement. The Sultan sat up alarmed, for the young man was his most skillful assistant.

"I must have your best horse!" the youth cried out. "There is little time! I must fly at once to Baghdad!"

The Sultan asked why the young man was in such a rush.

"Because," came the hurried reply, "just now, as I was walking in the palace garden, I saw Death standing there. And when Death saw me, he raised his arms in a frightening motion. Oh, it was horrible! I must escape at once!"

The Sultan quickly arranged for the youth to have his fastest horse. And no sooner had the young man thundered out through the palace gate, than the Sultan himself went into the garden. Death was still there.

The Sultan was angry. "What do you mean?" he demanded. "What do you mean by raising your arms and frightening my young friend?"

"Your Majesty," Death said calmly, "I did not mean to frighten him. You see, I raised my arms only in surprise. I was astonished to see him here in your garden, for I have an appointment with him tonight in Baghdad."

❧ What do you suppose might have happened if the young man had stayed at the Sultan's palace instead of going to Baghdad?

153

•❖ How might a person change his or her destiny? Write your own short tale about someone who tries.

_____

_____

_____

_____

_____

_____

_____

_____

_____

_____

_____

_____

_____

_____

Good readers understand that characters' struggles against destiny are a way to make us examine human nature.

Four
A Different Drummer

If a man does not keep pace with his companions, perhaps it is because he hears a different drummer. — Henry David Thoreau

Some **characters** step to a different drummer. In following their own beliefs, they come into conflict with society. Their struggles may involve efforts to gain acceptance, to understand the values of another culture, to establish their own identity, or to correct injustices. Writers include these types of struggles in their work not only to explore conflict but also to reveal important aspects of character.

In this selection, Mary Whitebird, a Kaw Indian, recalls a conflict from her own childhood. As you read the excerpt, think about how the conflict reveals important information about Mary's character.

from "Ta-Na-E-Ka" by Mary Whitebird

As my birthday drew closer, I had awful nightmares about it. I was reaching the age at which all Kaw Indians had to participate in Ta-Na-E-Ka. Well, not all Kaws. Many of the younger families on the reservation were beginning to give up the old customs. But my grandfather, Amos Deer Leg, was devoted to tradition. He still wore handmade beaded moccasins instead of shoes, and kept his iron gray hair in tight braids. He could speak English, but he spoke it only with white men. With his family he used a Sioux dialect.

Grandfather was one of the last living Indians (he died in 1953 when he was eighty-one) who actually fought against the U.S. Cavalry. Not only did he fight, he was wounded in a skirmish at Rose Creek—a famous encounter in which the celebrated Kaw chief Flat Nose lost his life. At the time, my grandfather was only eleven years old.

Eleven was a magic word among the Kaws. It was the time of Ta-Na-E-Ka, the "flowering of adulthood." It was the age, my grandfather informed us hundreds of times, "when a boy could prove himself to be a warrior and a girl took the first steps to womanhood."

"I don't want to be a warrior," my cousin, Roger Deer Leg, confided to me. "I'm going to become an accountant."

"None of the other tribes make girls go through the endurance ritual," I complained to my mother.

"It won't be as bad as you think, Mary," my mother said, ignoring my protests. "Once you've gone through it, you'll certainly never forget it. You'll be proud."

Response notes

155

from **"Ta-Na-E-Ka"** by Mary Whitebird

I even complained to my teacher, Mrs. Richardson, feeling that, as a white woman, she would side with me.

She didn't. "All of us have rituals of one kind or another," Mrs. Richardson said. "And look at it this way: how many girls have the opportunity to compete on equal terms with boys? Don't look down on your heritage."

Heritage, indeed! I had no intention of living on a reservation for the rest of my life. I was a good student. I loved school. My fantasies were about knights in armor and fair ladies in flowing gowns being saved from dragons. It never once occurred to me that being Indian was exciting.

●◆ Recall a time when you "heard a different drummer," or felt at odds with social or cultural expectations. Describe your experience in a short paragraph.

●◆ Describe the **narrator** of the story and what we learn about her character as a result of the conflict she faces.

....

....

....

....

....

●◆ How might the narrator resolve the conflict she describes? Write a letter to the narrator of "Ta-Na-E-Ka." Offer your opinion or advice to help her resolve the conflict.

....

....

157

....

....

....

....

....

....

....

....

....

....

Conflicts
between characters and
society often reveal information
about the characters' motivations,
values, and personality
traits.

Five

Against the Elements

As every true-life adventure fan knows, a battle against nature makes a riveting story. Tales of wilderness survival, of harrowing treks by land or sea, and of floods, storms, and other natural disasters all abound with the suspense that keeps us reading. A character's conflicts with nature also reveal his or her personality. In a battle against the elements, traits such as competence and incompetence, wisdom and foolishness, cowardice and courage stand out.

This excerpt from *Dragonwings* revolves around a natural disaster—the San Francisco earthquake of 1906. Moonshadow and his father are Chinese immigrants; Miss Whitlaw is their American landlady; and Robin is the landlady's niece. As you read, mark examples of characters vs. nature.

Response notes

from *Dragonwings* by Laurence Yep

A strange, eerie silence hung over the city. The bells had stilled in their steeples, and houses had stopped collapsing momentarily. It was as if the city itself were holding its breath. Then we could hear the hissing of gas from the broken pipes, like dozens of angry snakes, and people, trapped inside the mounds, began calling. Their voices sounded faint and ghostly, as if dozens of ghosts floated over the rubble, crying in little, distant voices for help. Robin and I pressed close to one another for comfort. It was Miss Whitlaw who saved us. It was she who gave us something important to do and brought us out of shock.

She pressed her lips together for a moment, as if she were deciding something. *"We must get those people out."*

"It would take four of us weeks to clear tunnels for them," Father said.

"We'll draft help. After all, we were put on this earth to help one another," Miss Whitlaw said.

Father suppressed a grin. *"I see what can do. But better put on clothes."*

"What? Oh, my." Miss Whitlaw was suddenly horrified to be found in her nightgown in public. *"Come, Robin."* She took her by the hand and practically pulled her up the steps.

Father shook his head affectionately. He sat down on a chest in the hall and he and I began braiding up his queue. On his advice, we both pinned our queues into tight buns at the back of our heads. When we got outside the house, though, Father stopped. "I've put my boots on the wrong feet." Sure enough, he had his left boot on his right foot and vice versa. We both laughed a little louder than the joke actually deserved, but we were just so relieved that we were still alive after the disaster. Father sat down on the sidewalk and got his boots on

from ***Dragonwings*** by Laurence Yep

Response notes

right. He stood up, stamping his feet back into his boots. Then we looked around.

We had gone to sleep on a street crowded with buildings, some three or four stories high and crowded with people; and now many of the houses were gone, and the ones that remained were dangerously close to falling too. There was a hole in the cobblestone street about a yard wide and twenty feet long. As we watched, a cobblestone fell over the edge, clattering ten feet to the bottom.

I heard one person compare it to being on the moon. It was that kind of desolate feeling—just looking at huge hills of rubble: of brick and broken wooden slats that had once been houses. On top of the piles we would see the random collection of things that had survived the quake: somebody's rag doll, an old bottle, a fiddle, the back of an upholstered chair . . . and a woman's slender wrist, sticking out of the rubble as if calling for help.

And then the survivors started to emerge, and I saw that there were as many hurt in mind as in body. Some people wandered out of the buildings almost naked, others still in their nightclothes. I saw one man with the lather on one side of his face, the other side already clean-shaven. In his hand was a lather-covered razor. One woman in a nightgown walked by, carrying her crying baby by its legs as if it were a dead chicken. Father caught her by the shoulder and gently took the baby from her.

"Fix her arms," Father told me. I set her arms so she could cradle the baby—as if the mother were a doll. Then Father put the baby back into her arms. She dumbly nodded her thanks and wandered on.

Other people who had taken the time to dress had dressed in the oddest things, choosing things they wanted to save rather than what would be appropriate for a disaster. I saw one shopgirl go by in a ball gown with the ruffles sounding crisp in the morning air. Perhaps she had saved for a year to buy it. I don't know. But I saw another man in formal tails go by. His wife carried the baby while he pushed a baby carriage filled with jewelry, a frying pan, and a candelabrum.

Then along came a big healthy man with ginger whiskers. He had slipped his trousers on over his red long johns. In his arms he had a chest.

Father tried to stop him. *"Please—need help."* Father pointed to the mound before us, from which the ghostly voices were calling.

"Be off with you," said the man.

Father tried grabbing him by his blue suspenders, but the man dodged away and started running.

159

●✦ In the chaos after the earthquake, several of Father's personality traits
are revealed. For each of his traits listed below, write details illustrating it,
taken from the selection. Then list one more trait that you notice in Father,
and add details from the selection to support it.

compassion

....

....

sense of humor

....

....

....

another trait: _____

....

....

....

●✦ Explain what Miss Whitlaw's actions after the earthquake reveal to you
about her character.

....

....

....

....

....

....

Critical
readers understand that a
conflict with nature creates suspense
and often reveals characters'
personalities.

Style and Structure

Everyone has his or her own style. Whatever yours is, you probably change it to fit the occasion. For example, you adapt your clothes and your speech to different situations. (You would probably wear different clothes to school than to a fancy party, and you might talk differently when you're with your friends than when you're in the principal's office.)

Writers, too, develop styles suited to particular audiences or situations. In this unit, you'll take a closer look at style (the choices that writers make when they compose) and structure (the way that writers organize their writing). You'll look at how and why writers make the choices they do. Not only will you gain a better understanding of what you read, you will also start to develop your own writing style.

One What Makes a Style?

Think about the authors that you enjoy reading. What draws you to them? You probably enjoy their **style**—the way they express ideas. Style involves choices like these:

- Does the writer use mostly short, simple sentences; more complex sentences; or a combination?
- Is the **narrator** directly involved in the story or on the outside?
- Is the language informal or formal? simple or complex?
- Does the writing include figurative expressions or simple **descriptions**?
- What **tone** works the best for the piece?

Now read two excerpts by two different authors. Jot down in the response notes how each writer might have answered the above "style questions." In this first excerpt from *The Call of the Wild*, Buck, part dog, part wolf, encounters a wolf.

Response Notes

from *The Call of the Wild* by Jack London

He had made no noise, yet it ceased from its howling and tried to sense his presence. Buck stalked into the open, half crouching, body gathered compactly together, tail straight and stiff, feet falling with unwonted care. Every movement advertised commingled threatening and overture of friendliness. It was the menacing truce that marks the meeting of wild beasts that prey. But the wolf fled at sight of him. He followed, with wild leapings, in a frenzy to overtake. He ran him into a blind channel, in the bed of the creek, where a timber jam barred the way. The wolf whirled about, pivoting on his hind legs after the fashion of Joe and of all cornered husky dogs, snarling and bristling, clipping his teeth together in a continuous and rapid succession of snaps.

Buck did not attack, but circled him about and hedged him in with friendly advances. The wolf was suspicious and afraid; for Buck made three of him in weight, while his head barely reached Buck's shoulder. Watching his chance, he darted away, and the chase was resumed. Time and again he was cornered, and the thing repeated, though he was in poor condition or Buck could not so easily have overtaken him. He would run till Buck's head was even with his flank, when he would whirl around at bay, only to dash away again at the first opportunity.

But in the end Buck's pertinacity was rewarded; for the wolf, finding that no harm was intended, finally sniffed noses with him. Then they became friendly, and played about in the nervous, half-coy way with which fierce beasts belie their fierceness. After some time of this the wolf started off at an easy lope in a manner that plainly showed he was going

from *The Call of the Wild* by Jack London

Response notes

somewhere. He made it clear to Buck that he was to come, and they ran side by side through the somber twilight, straight up the creek bed, into the gorge from which it issued, and across the bleak divide where it took its rise.

On the opposite slope of the watershed they came down into a level country where were great stretches of forest and many streams, and through these great stretches they ran steadily, hour after hour, the sun rising higher and the day growing warmer. Buck was wildly glad. He knew he was at last answering the call, running by the side of his wood brother toward the place from where the call surely came. Old memories were coming upon him fast, and he was stirring to them as of old he stirred to the realities of which they were the shadows. He had done this thing before, somewhere in that other and dimly remembered world, and he was doing it again, now, running free in the open, the unpacked earth underfoot, the wide sky overhead.

> In the following excerpt, a young girl named Karana is alone on an island after all of her tribe leaves. In this excerpt, Karana tries to leave the island for the mainland.

from *Island of the Blue Dolphins* by Scott O'Dell

At dusk I looked back. The Island of the Blue Dolphins had disappeared. This was the first time that I felt afraid.

There were only hills and valleys of water around me now. When I was in a valley I could see nothing and when the canoe rose out of it, only the ocean stretching away and away.

Night fell and I drank from the basket. The water cooled my throat.

The sea was black and there was no difference between it and the sky. The waves made no sound among themselves, only faint noises as they went under the canoe or struck against it. Sometimes the noises seemed angry and at other times like people laughing. I was not hungry because of my fear.

The first star made me feel less afraid. It came out low in the sky and it was in front of me, toward the east. Other stars began to appear all around, but it was this one I kept my gaze upon. It was in the figure that we call a serpent, a star which shone green and which I knew. Now and then it was hidden by mist, yet it always came out brightly again.

Without this star I would have been lost, for the waves never changed. They came always from the same direction and in a manner that kept pushing me away from the place I wanted to reach. For this reason the canoe made a path in the black water like a snake. But somehow I kept moving toward the star which shone in the east.

What style choices did Jack London and Scott O'Dell make? Use the chart below to compare and contrast their styles.

Style Choice	Jack London	Scott O'Dell
Point of view	3rd person—told by someone outside the story	
Length of sentences		
Type of language (informal or formal? simple or complex?)		
Are there figurative expressions, such as similes and metaphors?		
Tone—how the writing "sounds" (suspenseful, scary, exciting, and so on)		

Go back to the excerpts and circle "proof" for one of the style choices.

●◆Which style did you find easier to read? Which did you like better? Imagine that you are on a planning committee for next year's seventh-grade class. Based on the excerpts, which book—*The Call of the Wild* or *Island of the Blue Dolphins*—do you think should be required reading? Why? Base part of your answer on the writer's style.

165

A writer makes choices about how to express ideas. These choices— about word choice, sentence length, and so on— make up the author's style.

Two A Poetic Style

Poets make the same kinds of style choices as writers of prose. Poets think carefully about style choices, because they try to express "large" ideas in small spaces. As you read "Chinese Hot Pot," ask yourself: What is the poet's attitude toward America? How does he express that attitude? Jot down the answers to these questions in the response notes. (*Dá bìn lóuh* is the Vietnamese word for the Chinese hot pot, a boiling pot of broth in which people cook meat, fish, poultry, and vegetables.)

Response notes

Chinese Hot Pot
Wing Tek Lum

My dream of America
is like *dá bìn lóuh*
with people of all persuasions and tastes
sitting down around a common pot
chopsticks and basket scoops here and there
some cooking squid and others beef
some tofu or watercress
all in one broth
like a stew that really isn't
as each one chooses what he wishes to eat
only that the pot and fire are shared
along with the good company
and the sweet soup
spooned out at the end of the meal.

166

◆What do you think of Wing Tek Lum's poem?

....

....

....

....

....

....

●◆ How does Wing Tek Lum express his attitude toward America? Use the "style checklist" to analyze Lum's style.

✓ The poem's tone is .... (happy, sad, angry, etc.)

✓ The words are .... (formal, informal, etc.)

✓ The impression that this poem gives is ....

....

✓ Lum's feeling about America is ....

....

●◆ How do you feel about America? Model your work on Lum's and write four or five lines for a poem of your own. Think about the style that you will use and how your words will express your feelings.

167

My dream of America

....

....

....

....

....

....

....

....

....

....

....

The style an author uses can reflect how the author feels about the subject.

Three
Dramatic Structure

Fade out . . . *The curtain rises . . . The character enters . . .* When you see these kinds of words in a piece of writing, you are probably reading *drama*, writing that is meant to be performed by actors in front of an audience. Although both dramas and short stories have **characters** and **plots**, a drama definitely looks different on the page.

The Inspector-General takes place during a time of harsh rule in late nineteenth-century Russia. (An inspector-general would travel to a town to make sure that the people who lived there were obeying the unjust laws of that time.) As you read the play, circle phrases, words, and other elements (such as stage directions) that you would not find in a short story.

← Response notes →

The Inspector-General by Anton Chekhov

The curtain goes up to reveal falling snow and a cart facing away from us. Enter the STORYTELLER, who begins to read the story. Meanwhile, the TRAVELER enters. He is a middle-aged man of urban appearance, wearing dark glasses and a long overcoat with its collar turned up. He is carrying a small traveling bag. He climbs into the cart and sits facing us.

STORYTELLER. The Inspector-General. In deepest incognito, first by express train, then along back roads, Pyotr Pavlovich Posudin was hastening toward the little town of N__, to which he had been summoned by an anonymous letter. "I'll take them by surprise," he thought to himself. "I'll come down on them like a thunderbolt out of the blue. I can just imagine their faces when they hear who I am." *(Enter the DRIVER, a peasant, who climbs onto the cart, so that he is sitting with his back to us, and the cart begins to trundle slowly away from us.)* And when he thought to himself for long enough, he fell into conversation with the driver of the cart. What did he talk about? About himself, of course. *(Exit the STORYTELLER.)*

TRAVELER. I gather you've got a new inspector-general in these parts.

DRIVER. True enough.

TRAVELER. Know anything about him? *(The DRIVER turns and looks at the TRAVELER, who turns his coat collar up a little higher.)*

DRIVER. Know anything about him? Of course we do! We know everything about all of them up there! Every last little clerk —we know the color of his hair and the size of his boots! *(He turns back to the front, and the TRAVELER permits himself a slight smile.)*

TRAVELER. So, what do you reckon? Any good, is he? *(The DRIVER turns around.)*

The Inspector-General by Anton Chekhov

DRIVER. Oh, yes, he's a good one, this one.

TRAVELER. Really?

DRIVER. Did one good thing straight off.

TRAVELER. What was that?

DRIVER. He got rid of the last one. Holy terror he was! Hear him coming five miles off! Let's say he's going to this little town. Somewhere like we're going, say. He'd let all the world know about it a month before. So now he's on his way, say, and it's like thunder and lightning coming down the road. And when he gets where he's going, he has a good sleep. He has a good eat and drink, and then he starts. Stamps his feet, shouts his head off. Then he has another good sleep, and off he goes.

TRAVELER. But the new one's not like that?

DRIVER. Oh, no. The new one goes everywhere on the quiet. Creeps around like a cat. Don't want no one to see him, don't want no one to know who he is. Say he's going into this town down the road here. Someone there sent him a letter on the sly, let's say. "Things going on here you should know about." Something of that kind. Well, now, he creeps out of his office, so none of them up there see him go. He hops on a train just like anyone else, just like you or me. When he gets off, he don't go jumping into a cab or nothing fancy. Oh, no. He wraps himself up from head to toe so you can't see his face, and he wheezes away like an old dog so no one can recognize his voice.

TRAVELER. Wheezes? That's not wheezing! That's the way he talks! So I gather.

DRIVER. Oh, is it? But the tales they tell about him. You'd laugh till you burst your tripes!

TRAVELER *(sourly).* I'm sure I would.

DRIVER. He drinks, mind!

TRAVELER *(startled).* Drinks?

DRIVER. Oh, like a hole in the ground. Famous for it.

TRAVELER. He's never touched a drop! I mean, from what I've heard.

DRIVER. Oh, not in public, no. Goes to some great ball—"No thank you, not for me." Oh, no, he puts it away at home! Wakes up in the morning, rubs his eyes, and the first thing he does, he shouts, "Vodka!" So in runs his valet with a glass. Fixed himself up a tube behind his desk, he has. Leans down, takes a pull on it, no one the wiser.

TRAVELER *(offended).* How do you know all this, may I ask?

DRIVER. Can't hide it from the servants, can you? The valet and the coachman have got tongues in their heads. Then again, he's on the road, say, going about his business, and he keeps the bottle in his little bag. (*The* TRAVELER

169

discreetly pushes the traveling bag out of the DRIVER'S sight.) And his housekeeper . . .

TRAVELER. What about her?

DRIVER. Runs circles around him, she does, like a fox round his tail. She's the one who wears the trousers. The people aren't half so frightened of him as they are of her.

TRAVELER. But at least he's good at his job, you say?

DRIVER. Oh, he's a blessing from heaven, I'll grant him that.

TRAVELER. Very cunning, you were saying.

DRIVER. Oh, he creeps around, all right.

TRAVELER. And then he pounces, yes? I should think some people must get the surprise of their life, mustn't they?

DRIVER. No, no. Let's be fair, now. Give him his due. He don't make no trouble.

TRAVELER. No. I mean, if no one knows he's coming . . .

DRIVER. Oh, that's what *he* thinks, but *we* all know.

TRAVELER. You know?

DRIVER. Oh, some gentleman gets off the train at the station back there with his greatcoat up to his eyebrows and says, "No, I don't want a cab, thank you. Just an ordinary horse and cart for me." Well, we'd put two and two together, wouldn't we? Say it was you, now, creeping along down the road here. The lads would be down there in a cab by now! By the time you got there, the whole town would be as regular as clockwork! And you'd think to yourself, "Oh, look at that! As clean as a whistle! And they didn't know I was coming!" No, that's why he's such a blessing after the other one. This one believes it.

TRAVELER. Oh, I see.

DRIVER. What, you thought we didn't know him? Why, we've got the electric telegraph these days! Take today, now. I'm going past the station back there this morning, and the fellow who runs the buffet comes out like a bolt of lightning. Arms full of baskets and bottles. "Where are you off to?" I say. "Doing drinks and refreshments for the inspector-general!" he says, and he jumps into a carriage and goes flying down the road here. So there's the inspector-general, all muffled up like a roll of carpet, going secretly along in a cart somewhere, and when he gets there, nothing to be seen but vodka and cold salmon!

TRAVELER *(shouts).* Turn around!

DRIVER *(to the horse).* Whoa, boy! Whoa! *(To the* TRAVELER.*)* Oh, so what's this, then? Don't want to go running into the inspector-general, is that it? *(The* TRAVELER *gestures impatiently for the* DRIVER *to turn the cart around.* DRIVER *to the horse.)* Back we go, then, boy. Home we go. *(He turns the cart around and the* TRAVELER *takes a swig*

The Inspector-General by Anton Chekhov

from his traveling bag.) Though if I know the old devil, he's like as not turned around and gone home again himself. *(Blackout).*

Response notes

The structure of *The Inspector-General* clues you in on when each character realizes what the other one knows. Return to the play and put an X in the margin when the driver realizes that his passenger is the inspector-general. Put a Y in the margin when the inspector-general realizes he has been found out.

●◆ What structural elements do dramas and short stories have in common? How are the two different? Use the Venn diagram to record your ideas. In the left circle, write elements that you would find in drama. Write down things that you would find in short stories in the right circle. Where the circles intersect, write elements you would find in both.

171

Drama

Short Story

A drama has a distinctive structure, which includes stage directions and character names set aside from the dialogue.

Style (the way ideas are expressed) and **structure** (the framework used for writing) work together like a team. All teams have a structure: a set number of players, a captain or leader, a system of rules, and so on. But different teams use different plays to be successful. Writing is the same way. Within certain frameworks, such as poetry, ideas can be expressed in many different ways.

Some poems have strict structures. Other poems, written in what's called **free verse**, don't follow rules for number and length of lines. But even a free verse poem has a structure. Poets decide, "How does the way this poem looks—the number of lines, the arrangement of lines, the spaces—convey the meaning of the poem?" As you read "Direction," decide how the structure of the poem reflects its meaning.

Direction
Alonzo Lopez

I was directed by my grandfather
To the East,
   so I might have the power of the bear;
To the South,
   so I might have the courage of the eagle;
To the West,
   so I might have the wisdom of the owl;
To the North,
   so I might have the craftiness of the fox;
To the Earth,
   so I might receive her fruit;
To the Sky,
   so I might lead a life of innocence.

Response notes

172

➡ How does the poem's structure reflect or enhance its meaning?

●◆ Use the style and structure of "Direction" as a model to write a poem about a time when someone important to you gave you advice.

Direction

My title:

I was directed by my grandfather

To the East,

    so I might have the power of the bear;

To the South,

    so I might have the courage of the eagle;

To the West,

    so I might have the wisdom of the owl;

To the North,

    so I might have the craftiness of the fox;

To the Earth,

    so I might receive her fruit;

To the Sky,

    so I might lead a life of innocence.

As you read a poem, examine its structure to figure out the reasons behind the writer's placement of words, lines, and stanzas.

173

Five Finding a Style and Structure

Writers understand that different purposes call for different **structures**. After all, you wouldn't write a business letter in the form of a poem. Writers also understand the importance of choosing a **style** and structure that best reflects how they feel about a subject. Readers, in turn, need to be aware of how style and structure can affect their understanding of what they read.

✏️ Now choose another style and structure to describe the same incident you wrote about in your poem in Lesson Four. Rewrite the incident using some other format—for example, a diary entry, the words from a telephone conversation, or a speech.

✏️ How does changing the style and structure of your piece change the writing? How does it change the way a reader might react to it?

Choose a style and structure for your own writing that will best reflect your feelings about the subject.

Active Reading: Poetry

The poet Naomi Shihab Nye once said, "Poetry looks *into* things, not just *at* them." Have you ever tried to "get into" a poem? It's easier than it sounds. Start by reading the poem straight through to get a sense of the whole poem. Then look at each word. Think about the meanings of the words, and how the poet puts those words together. When you actively read a poem this way, a group of words is transformed into something that has meaning, detailing a single moment of understanding or even an entire lifetime of experiences. In the lessons in this unit, you will learn strategies that poets use to transform words into messages, strategies that you can use to "get into" poetry.

Reading a poem is like putting a puzzle together. The poet carefully chooses words, sounds, images, ideas, and feelings. Then you, the reader, fit the "pieces" together into something that has meaning. What can you do to put the pieces into place? Here are some strategies to try:

• Look at the title of the poem. What does the title say about the poem or its meaning?

• Read the poem straight through to get a feel for it. Reread to figure out any confusing parts.

• Try to **visualize** what's happening in the poem.

• Circle ideas or images that are confusing. Then you can go back to figure out what they mean.

• Restate each line or **stanza** in your own words to see if you understand it.

Use these strategies as you read "The Funeral." Put explanations and questions in the response notes.

Response notes

The Funeral
Gordon Parks

After many snows I was home again.
Time had whittled down to mere hills
The great mountains of my childhood.
Raging rivers I once swam trickled now
           like gentle streams.
And the wide road curving on to China or
          Kansas City or perhaps Calcutta,
Had withered to a crooked path of dust
Ending abruptly at the county burying ground.
Only the giant who was my father
           remained the same.
A hundred strong men strained beneath his coffin
When they bore him to his grave.

Which strategies did you use to understand the poem? Go back to the list of strategies and circle the ones that were most helpful to you.

Reread the last four lines of the poem. The speaker's father probably did not need a hundred men to carry his coffin. So what do these lines mean? Write them in your own words.

One of the messages of "The Funeral" is the way in which the passage of time affects the speaker and his perceptions. How does the speaker see his home differently now than when he was a boy? Use the chart below to record ideas from the poem.

Objects/People	Childhood View	Adult View
hills		
rivers		
road		
father		

177

Use active reading strategies such as restating ideas in your own words and figuring out what images mean. These will help you understand the ideas in a poem.

Understanding a poem is almost like solving a math problem. There are two parts to the equation that equal "understanding." One part is what the poet commits to the page—the words, sounds, and images. The other part is what the reader brings to the poem. Only you can decide how a poem speaks to you. Try using these ideas to respond to poems:

- Read a poem straight through without stopping to "analyze" it.

- Read it again. Ask yourself, "What do I think of the poem? What do I like about it?"

- Think it through. Ask yourself, "What does the poem say to me? When have I ever been in a situation like this? How am I like the speaker of the poem? What do I think of the speaker?"

As you read the following poem, make notes about your responses in the margin.

Response notes

There's This That I Like About Hockey, My Lad
John Kieran

There's this that I like about hockey, my lad;
   It's a clattering, battering sport.
As a popular pastime it isn't half bad
   For chaps of the sturdier sort.
You step on the gas and you let in the clutch;
You start on a skate and come back on a crutch;
Your chance of surviving is really not much;
   It's something like storming a fort.

There's this I like about hockey, my boy;
   There's nothing about it that's tame.
The whistle is blown and the players deploy;
   They start in to maul and to maim.
There's a dash at the goal and a crash on the ice;
The left wing goes down when you've swatted him twice;
And your teeth by a stick are removed in a trice;
   It's really a rollicking game.

There's this that I like about hockey, old chap;
   I think you'll agree that I'm right;
Although you may get an occasional rap,
   There's always good fun in the fight.
So toss in the puck, for the players are set;
Sing ho! for the dash on the enemy net;
And ho! for the smash as the challenge is met;
   And hey! for a glorious night!

◖◗ What sport or activity do you feel strongly about? How do your feelings compare to the speaker's?

◖◗ Return to the list of ideas for responding to poems on page 178. Choose two questions from the list and answer them in the space below.

When you read a poem, think about your personal response to it. Connecting to the poem will help you better understand and enjoy it.

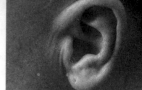

How a Poem Sounds

$$S$$ome poems invite you to read them aloud. Remember listening to, and then reading, nursery rhymes when you were little? What made them so fun was not just their subjects, but the way they sounded. Poets use techniques called sound devices to add meaning to their work:

Rhyme
Rhyming words end with the same sound, such as *lake* and *cake*. Rhyme can happen at the end or in the middle of lines of poems.

Rhythm
Rhythm is the beat of a poem. Some poems sound just like conversation (these are called *free verse*), while others have a set pattern.

Repetition
Some poems repeat words, phrases, or stanzas to draw attention to certain subjects or ideas.

Read "Annabel Lee" through once for meaning. Then reread the poem and circle instances in which Edgar Allan Poe uses rhyme, rhythm, or repetition. In the response notes, jot down the effect of the sound device.

Response notes

Repeating love and loved—shows speaker's strong feelings

Annabel Lee
Edgar Allan Poe

It was many and many a year ago,
    In a kingdom by the sea,
That a maiden there lived whom you may know
    By the name of Annabel Lee;
And this maiden she lived with no other thought
    Than to (love) and be (loved) by me.

I was a child and *she* was a child,
    In this kingdom by the sea:
But we loved with a love that was more than love—
    I and my Annabel Lee—
With a love that the winged seraphs of heaven
    Coveted her and me.

And this was the reason that, long ago,
    In this kingdom by the sea,
A wind blew out of a cloud, chilling
    My beautiful Annabel Lee;
So that her highborn kinsmen came
    And bore her away from me,
To shut her up in a sepulcher
    In this kingdom by the sea.

The angels, not half so happy in heaven,
    Went envying her and me—
Yes!—that was the reason (as all men know,
    In this kingdom by the sea)
That the wind came out of the cloud by night,
    Chilling and killing my Annabel Lee.

But our love it was stronger by far than the love
    Of those who were older than we—
    Of many far wiser than we—
And neither the angels in heaven above,
    Nor the demons down under the sea,
Can ever dissever my soul from the soul
    Of the beautiful Annabel Lee—

For the moon never beams, without bringing me dreams
    Of the beautiful Annabel Lee;
And the stars never rise, but I feel the bright eyes
    Of the beautiful Annabel Lee;
And so, all the night-tide, I lie down by the side
Of my darling—my darling—my life and my bride,
    In the sepulcher there by the sea,
    In her tomb by the sounding sea.

Response notes

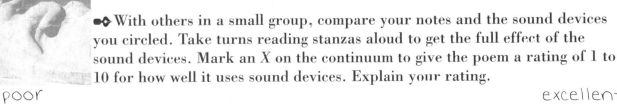

●◆ With others in a small group, compare your notes and the sound devices
you circled. Take turns reading stanzas aloud to get the full effect of the
sound devices. Mark an X on the continuum to give the poem a rating of 1 to
10 for how well it uses sound devices. Explain your rating.

poor   excellent
1 ◀───▶ **10**

Reasons:

....

....

....

....

....

....

◗◆ In what other ways could the speaker express his feelings? Rewrite the poem in another form, such as a letter, a dialogue between friends, or a telegram. When you are finished, compare your writing to the poem.

◗◆ Which format do you think is more moving for readers, the poem or the format you chose to write in? Explain.

Use the sound devices you encounter in poetry to determine what ideas the writer is trying to emphasize.

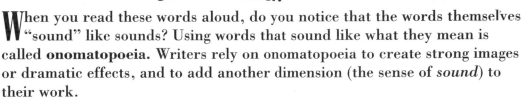

Four
Sound Effects

Crash!   Boom!   Sizzle.   Slither.   Hissss...

When you read these words aloud, do you notice that the words themselves "sound" like sounds? Using words that sound like what they mean is called **onomatopoeia**. Writers rely on onomatopoeia to create strong images or dramatic effects, and to add another dimension (the sense of *sound*) to their work.

When you read a poem, it helps to read it aloud. Think to yourself, "What effects is the writer trying to achieve with sound?" As you read "Cynthia in the Snow," put an *X* in the response notes near any instances of onomatopoeia.

Cynthia in the Snow
Gwendolyn Brooks

It SHUSHES.
It hushes
The loudness in the road.
It flitter-twitters,
And laughs away from me.
It laughs a lovely
    whiteness,
And whitely whirs away,
To be
Some otherwhere,
Still white as milk or shirts.
So beautiful it hurts.

Response notes

183

➥How does the onomatopoeia in this poem make you feel? Which line from "Cynthia in the Snow" do you like most? Why?

....

....

....

....

....

Noise is all around us. Sit in a place for 10 minutes (such as a playground, the cafeteria, or a shopping mall) and do nothing but listen. Without naming the place, write a poem about it, using onomatopoeia to describe the noises you heard. Can someone reading the poem tell what place you are describing?

184

Writers use onomatopoeia to create precise images and dramatic sound effects in poetry.

Five

A Figure of Speech

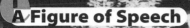

"The lightning stretched its fiery arms toward the earth."

Can lightning really stretch itself toward earth? When writers give non-human things human characteristics (such as the ability to speak, human body parts, or feelings), they are using a figure of speech called **personification**. Personification can make a poem interesting to read. It can also help readers by presenting things that are hard to understand in familiar ways.

The following poem, Paul Fleischman's "Chrysalis Diary," is meant to be read aloud by two readers at once. (A *chrysalis* is the stage between a caterpillar and a moth or butterfly.) You may want to read the poem aloud with a partner first. Then jot down notes about personification as you reread the poem.

Chrysalis Diary
Paul Fleischman

November 13:

Cold told me
to fasten my feet
to this branch,

to dangle upside down
from my perch,

to shed my skin,

to cease being a caterpillar
and I have obeyed.

and I have obeyed.

December 6:

Green,

the color of leaves and life,
has vanished!

has vanished!
The empire of leaves
lies in ruins!

lies in ruins!
I study the
brown new world around me.

I fear the future.

I hear few sounds.

Have any others of my kind
survived this cataclysm?

Swinging back and forth
in the wind,
I feel immeasurably alone.

January 4:

I can make out snow falling.

For five days and nights
it's been drifting down.

Response notes

Cold can talk.

185

CHRYSALIS DIARY (continued)

I find I never tire of
watching the flakes
in their multitudes
passing my window.

Astounding.
I enter these
wondrous events
in my chronicle

The world is now white.
Astounding.

knowing no reader
would believe me.

February 12:

Unable to see out
at all this morning.

and branches falling.

An ice storm last night.

Yet I hear boughs cracking

Hungry for sounds
in this silent world,
I cherish these,

ponder their import,

miser them away
in my memory,
and wait for more.

and wait for more.

March 28:

I wonder whether
I am the same being
who started this diary.

like the weather without.

my legs are dissolving,

I've felt stormy inside

My mouth is reshaping,

wings are growing
my body's not mine.

my body's not mine.
This morning,
a breeze from the south,
strangely fragrant,

a red-winged blackbird's
call in the distance,

a faint glimpse of green
In the branches.

And now I recall
that last night
I dreamt of flying.

●◆ What human qualities does the writer give to the chrysalis? Make a web to record these characteristics.

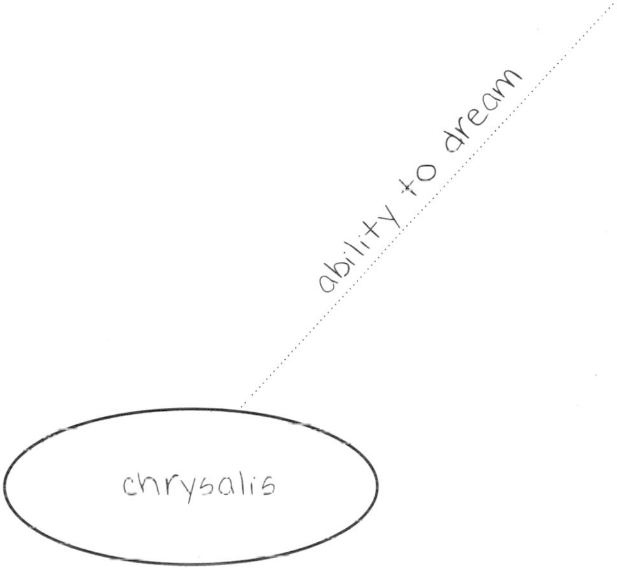

ability to dream

chrysalis

●◆ Caterpillars and butterflies are often the topics of textbooks, not poems. Think of another typical "textbook topic" and personify it in a poem.

Poets often use personification to present unfamiliar ideas in familiar ways.

Active Reading: Persuasive Writing

Writing a persuasive piece is like building a block tower. If you choose the biggest, sturdiest blocks, your tower will be tall and strong. The same thing is true for persuasive writing. If you build your argument using only the "sturdiest" persuasive techniques, your argument will be solid and strong.

In this unit, you'll explore five techniques that persuasive writers routinely use in their writing. Some of the techniques you'll practice using include:

- stating a clear opinion
- using facts to support your opinion
- choosing words that appeal to readers' emotions
- using tone to persuade

One The Viewpoint

Every piece of persuasive writing begins with an issue or topic and the author's viewpoint on that issue or topic. What does the author want to persuade us of? What does the writer want us to think or do? This is the author's **viewpoint**. For example, say that you are reading a newspaper and come across this headline: "My View on Year-Round School." The headline tells you the topic of the editorial: year-round school. You'll have to read the editorial to find out what the author's viewpoint or opinion is. Does the author approve of or disapprove of year-round school?

Read "Our Juvenile Curfew Is Working." Underline any clues you find about the author and his viewpoint.

190

"Our Juvenile Curfew Is Working" by Marc H. Morial

When I took office in May 1994, New Orleans had an out-of-control crime problem. Children were dying, citizens did not feel safe in their own homes, the numbers were staggering. Crime had become too personal, and familiar. As mayor, I knew that I could not solve this enormous problem alone. The only effective solution was a community solution.

Our vision was to save our city and its future generations. It was in this spirit that we developed the idea for the Juvenile Curfew Law. Curfew hours are from 8 p.m. to 6 a.m. Sunday through Thursday and from 11 p.m. to 6 a.m. Friday and Saturday. They are applicable to those under the age of 17. The Curfew Center is operational during those curfew hours. Our plan was to implement a curfew as a parent would lay down a house rule. Our curfew holds both the juvenile and the parent accountable. Parents are required to pick up their children from the Curfew Center and participate in counseling sessions. Repeat offenders' parents are issued a court summons and could risk being fined for failure to keep their children from violating curfew.

This "forced responsibility" is working. After 60 days of implementation, juvenile crime during curfew hours had decreased by 38 percent. After 90 days, overall crime had dropped by 14.6 percent. The crimes most significantly affected were armed robbery (down 29 percent), auto theft (down 28 percent) and murder (down 26 percent) as compared with the summer of 1993.

"Our Juvenile Curfew Is Working" by Marc H. Morial

This isn't just another cold, calculating law that does more harm than good. When the law was written, every consideration was given to our children. Curfew violators are not taken to jail. Our Curfew Center is for juvenile curfew offenders only, and the facility is freshly painted and brightly lit. The juvenile is checked in and taken to the Center's counseling area while the youth's parents are contacted. The objective is to open lines of communication, begin a dialogue between the parent and the child, and we hope, set new ground rules within the home. A 24-hour Curfew Hotline is available to answer questions about curfew policy and enforcement.

We have also constructed alternatives for young people by revitalizing the New Orleans Recreation Department (NORD), expanding its programs by more than 300 percent. The number of NORD summer camps increased from 17 to 41, serving more than 10,000 youths. The number of swimming pools went from four to 14. We created 1,300 new summer jobs for youths and secured $1.8 million in federal grants for AmeriCorps and Youth Action Corps. We are not just saying "No" to our youth. We are recreating dreams.

Some may say that we have overstepped the boundaries—that it is not our responsibility to become involved in personal family situations. I see it differently. The ultimate civil liberty is the right to be secure in our own homes, to feel safe in our streets, to have confidence that our children can go to school safely. If we do not step in and redirect our city and the families who live in it, then who will? We have taken every precaution to protect the legal, individual and constitutional rights of every citizen affected by the curfew regardless of age.

However, we will continue to defend our right to safety with every ounce of energy and spirit.

The statistics prove our curfew is working. This new law is keeping youths off the street and out of trouble. It is helping families be more responsive to one another and more responsive to their communities.

We are fighting crime with aggressive visionary programs supported by the whole community. We know that the country is watching. Jurisdictions across America have written or called asking how they can implement a similar law. Each day brings proof that a unified community with a vision and the energy to work tirelessly can do anything.

191

➤ What is Marc Morial's viewpoint on teen curfews?

➤ Do you share Morial's view on curfews? Write him a short letter explaining your opinion on curfews.

192

When you evaluate a piece of persuasive writing, start by identifying the author's viewpoint.

Two **The Support**

Persuasive writing is made up of a series of facts and opinions. A **fact** is something that is known to be true: *Social studies is a school subject.* An **opinion** is someone's personal beliefs about a topic: *Social studies is an interesting school subject.* Most persuasive writers rely on facts to support their opinions: *Nine out of ten seventh-graders say social studies is an interesting subject.*

Reread Morial's argument. Use a red pen to underline statements of fact and a blue pen to underline statements of opinion. Notice how his opinions are supported by facts:

Opinion: The juvenile curfew is working.

Fact: Juvenile crime is down 38% during curfew hours.

Fact: Auto theft is down 28%.

Fact: Armed robbery is down 29%.

Think of an issue or topic that is controversial in your town. Decide your opinion on the issue. Then think of three facts to support your opinion.

Opinion:

Fact:

Fact:

Fact:

193

●◆ Now use your graphic to write a paragraph about the issue you chose.
First express your opinion; then support it with facts.

....

....

....

....

....

....

....

....

194

....

....

....

....

....

....

....

....

....

When
you read persuasive
writing, look for facts that
support the author's
opinion.

Three

The Language

Persuasive writers often use loaded words in their arguments. Loaded words are words that give a strong suggestion of the author's opinion or perspective. They are meant to convince you, the reader, to embrace the author's perspective. For example, consider the difference between the words *filled* and *jammed*. The two words mean close to the same thing, but the word *jammed* is full of hidden meanings and implications. If the school cafeteria is "filled," it means there's a good-size crowd eating lunch. If it's "jammed," it means you might need to make other lunch plans.

Read this excerpt from Roger Ebert's review of the 1997 movie *Titanic*. Underline all of the loaded words you find.

from "Titanic" by Roger Ebert

Like a great iron Sphinx on the ocean floor, the Titanic faces still toward the West, interrupted forever on its only voyage. We see it in the opening shots of *Titanic*, encrusted with the silt of 85 years; a remote-controlled TV camera snakes its way inside, down corridors and through doorways, showing us staterooms built for millionaires and inherited by crustaceans.

These shots strike precisely the right note; the ship calls from its grave for its story to be told, and if the story is made of showbiz and hype, smoke and mirrors—well, so was the Titanic. She was "the largest work of man in all history," a character boasts, neatly dismissing the Pyramids and the Great Wall. There is a shot of her, early in the film, sweeping majestically beneath the camera from bow to stern, nearly 900 feet long and "unsinkable," it was claimed, until an iceberg made an irrefutable reply.

James Cameron's 194-minute, $200 million film of the tragic voyage is in the tradition of the great Hollywood epics. It is flawlessly crafted, intelligently constructed, strongly acted and spellbinding. If its story stays well within the traditional formulas for such pictures, well, you don't choose the most expensive film ever made as your opportunity to reinvent the wheel.

We know before the movie begins that certain things must happen. We must see the Titanic sail and sink, and be convinced we are looking at a real ship. There must be a human story—probably a romance—involving a few of the passengers. There must be vignettes involving some of the rest and a subplot involving the arrogance and pride of the ship's builders—and per-

Response notes

from "Titanic" by Roger Ebert

haps also their courage and dignity. And there must be a reenactment of the ship's terrible death throes; it took two and a half hours to sink, so that everyone aboard had time to know what was happening, and to consider their actions.

All of those elements are present in Cameron's *Titanic*, weighted and balanced like ballast, so that the film always seems in proportion. The ship was made out of models (large and small), visual effects and computer animation. You know intellectually that you're not looking at a real ocean liner—but the illusion is convincing and seamless. The special effects don't call inappropriate attention to themselves but get the job done.

What's your response to Ebert's review? Does he make you want to rush out to the video store to grab a copy of *Titanic*? Why or why not?

....

....

....

....

....

....

....

....

....

➨ Which words in Ebert's review would you say are "loaded"? Make a note of them on the web below. Add more spokes if you need to.

Majestic

Ebert's loaded words

➨ Now finish this sentence: Ebert's loaded words make his review

more / less _____ .
(circle one)

➨ Explain below why you completed the sentence the way you did.

_____

_____

_____

_____

_____

_____

Persuasive writers use loaded words in order to make their arguments more effective.

Four — The Emotional Appeal

One of the most effective forms of persuasive writing is the type that appeals to your emotions. This is the kind of writing that makes you feel angry or sad or joyous and in so doing convinces you to share the writer's opinion. Persuasive writers appeal to a reader's emotions in two ways:

1. They tell a story or give an example that makes the reader feel sad or happy or angry or any other emotion.

2. They adjust the **tone** of the writing so that it matches the emotions the writer wants us to feel.

Let's consider telling a story first. If a writer were to tell you a story about a child who goes without dinner night after night, you might be persuaded to donate money or food or do whatever else it would take to help the child. You react quickly because the writer has touched an emotional chord in you.

Read the first part of "Homeless," an essay by Anna Quindlen. As you read, watch for parts that appeal to your emotions.

Response notes

"Homeless" by Anna Quindlen

Her name was Ann, and we met in the Port Authority Bus Terminal several Januarys ago. I was doing a story on homeless people. She said I was wasting my time talking to her, she was just passing through, although she'd been passing through for more than two weeks. To prove to me that this was true, she rummaged through a tote bag and a manila envelope and finally unfolded a sheet of typing paper and brought out her photographs.

They were not pictures of family, or friends, or even a dog or cat, its eyes brown-red in the flashbulb's light. They were pictures of a house. It was like a thousand houses in a hundred towns, not suburb, not city, but somewhere in between, with aluminum siding and a chain link fence, a narrow driveway running up to a one-car garage and a patch of backyard. The house was yellow. I looked on the back for a date or a name, but neither was there. There was no need for discussion. I knew what she was trying to tell me, for it was something I had often felt. She was not adrift, alone, anonymous, although her bags and her raincoat with the grime shadowing its creases had made me believe she was. She had a house, or at least once upon a time had had one. Inside were curtains, a couch, a stove, pot holders. You are where you live. She was somebody.

Response notes

"Homeless" by Anna Quindlen

I've never been very good at looking at the big picture, taking the global view, and I've always been a person with an overactive sense of place, the legacy of an Irish grand-father. So it is natural that the thing that seems most wrong with the world to me right now is that there are so many people with no homes. I'm not simply talking about shelter from the elements, or three square meals a day or a mailing address to which the welfare people can send the check—although I know that all these are important for survival. I'm talking about a home, about precisely those kinds of feelings that have wound up in cross-stitch and French knots on samplers over the years.

●◆ What emotions did you feel as you were reading this part of Quindlen's article? Sketch an image or two that illustrates how you felt while reading "Homeless."

●◆ How effective was Quindlen's emotional appeal? Explain why you do or do not think this selection is persuasive.

....

....

....

....

....

....

Persuasive writers often tell stories or give examples designed to appeal to our emotions.

The Tone

Telling a story or giving an example is one way persuasive writers can appeal to readers' emotions. Another way is to modify the tone of the writing. **Tone** is the writer's attitude toward a subject. A writer's tone can be sarcastic or humorous or mournful or anything else. In a persuasive piece, the writer's tone will give you strong clues about how you, the reader, are supposed to respond.

Read the rest of "Homeless." Make notes about Quindlen's tone as you read.

Response notes

"warm and fuzzy"

"Homeless" (continued) by Anna Quindlen

Home is where the heart is. There's no place like it. I love my home with a ferocity totally out of proportion to its appearance or location. I love dumb things about it: the hot-water heater, the plastic rack you drain dishes in, the roof over my head, which occasionally leaks. And yet it is precisely those dumb things that make it what it is—a place of certainty, stability, predictability, privacy, for me and for my family. It is where I live. What more can you say about a place than that? That is everything.

Yet it is something that we have been edging away from gradually during my lifetime and the lifetimes of my parents and grandparents. There was a time when where you lived often was where you worked and where you grew the food you ate and even where you were buried. When that era passed, where you lived at least was where your parents had lived and where you would live with your children when you became enfeebled. Then, suddenly, where you lived was where you lived for three years, until you could move on to something else and something else again.

And so we have come to something else again, to children who do not understand what it means to go to their rooms because they have never had a room, to men and women whose fantasy is a wall they can paint a color of their own choosing, to old people reduced to sitting on molded plastic chairs, their skin blue-white in the lights of a bus station, who pull pictures of houses out of their bags. Homes have stopped being homes. Now they are real estate.

People find it curious that those without homes would rather sleep sitting up on benches or huddled in doorways than go to shelters. Certainly some prefer to do so because they are emotionally ill, because they have been

"Homeless" (continued) by Anna Quindlen

Response notes

locked in before and they are damned if they will be locked in again. Others are afraid of the violence and trouble they may find there. But some seem to want something that is not available in shelters, and they will not compromise, not for a cot, or oatmeal, or a shower with special soap that kills the bugs. "One room," a woman with a baby who was sleeping on her sister's floor, once told me, "painted blue." That was the crux of it; not size or location, but pride of ownership. Painted blue.

This is a difficult problem, and some wise and compassionate people are working hard at it. But in the main I think we work around it, just as we walk around it when it is lying on the sidewalk or sitting in the bus terminal— the problem, that is. It has been customary to take people's pain and lessen our own participation in it by turning it into an issue, not a collection of human beings. We turn an adjective into a noun: the poor, not poor people; the homeless, not Ann or the man who lives in the box or the woman who sleeps on the subway grate.

Sometimes I think we would be better off if we forgot about the broad strokes and concentrated on the details. Here is a woman without a bureau. There is a man with no mirror, no wall to hang it on. They are not the homeless. They are people who have no homes. No drawer that holds the spoons. No window to look out upon the world. My God. That is everything.

➡️ Consider Quindlen's tone and how she creates it. Read these four quotations from her essay. Underneath each quotation, explain how the words make you feel.

1. "Home is where the heart is."

   I feel:
   ....
   ....

2. "I love my home with a ferocity totally out of proportion to its appearance or location. I love dumb things about it: the hot water heater, the plastic rack you drain dishes in...."

   I feel:
   ....
   ....

3. "Here is a woman without a bureau. There is a man with no mirror, no wall to hang it on."

   I feel:
   ....

202

....

4. "My God. That is everything."

   I feel:
   ....
   ....

➡️ Now decide: what is Quindlen's tone in this essay? How does her tone make you feel as you read?

....
....
....
....

In a persuasive piece, the writer's tone will give you strong clues about how you, the reader, are supposed to feel.

© GREAT SOURCE. ALL RIGHTS RESERVED.

Focus on the Writer: Ray Bradbury

Readers of all ages consider Ray Bradbury a master storyteller. What's so masterful about Bradbury? What is it that people like about him? Why do both children and adults return to their favorite Bradbury stories over and over again?

For starters, Bradbury's characters are fascinating, his settings are amazing, and his plots are out of this world. He also has a knack for moving his readers back and forth between the real world and imaginary worlds without ever losing momentum—or the reader's interest.

In this unit, you'll have a chance to see Ray Bradbury the storyteller at work. By looking at a variety of Bradbury's works, you'll gain insights into his style and craft, as well as some of his themes and ideas.

In a fantasy, the writer creates an imaginary world and then asks readers to believe—at least for a little while—that this world really exists. To make it easier for the reader to believe, fantasy writers usually give their imaginary worlds some real-world features. For example, a fantasy writer might make up a story about cats who talk, laugh, and fly (imaginary world), but who also love chasing yarn balls and eating canned fish (real world).

In his fantasy stories, Bradbury always offers a mixture of real and imaginary. Most often he shows this mix in his **characters**—the people, animals, and "things" that inhabit his pages.

Begin your focus on Bradbury by reading this selection from the short story "Uncle Einar." As you read, keep an eye on the characters. What are their real qualities? What are their imaginary qualities? Write your comments in the response notes.

RESPONSE NOTES

204

from "Uncle Einar" by Ray Bradbury

"It will take only a minute," said Uncle Einar's sweet wife.

"I refuse," he said. "And that takes but a *second*."

"I've worked all morning," she said, holding to her slender back, "and you won't help? It's drumming for a rain."

"Let it rain," he cried, morosely. "I'll not be pierced by lightning just to air your clothes."

"But you're so quick at it."

"Again, I refuse." His vast tarpaulin wings hummed nervously behind his indignant back.

She gave him a slender rope on which were tied four dozen fresh-washed clothes. He turned it in his fingers with distaste. "So it's come to this," he muttered, bitterly. "To this, to this, to this." He almost wept angry and acid tears.

"Don't cry; you'll wet them down again," she said. "Jump up, now, run them about."

"Run them about." His voice was hollow, deep, and terribly wounded. "I say: let it thunder, let it pour!"

"If it was a nice, sunny day I wouldn't ask," she said, reasonably. "All my washing gone for nothing if you don't. They'll hang about the house—"

That *did* it. Above all, he hated clothes flagged and festooned so a man had to creep under on the way across a room. He jumped up. His vast green wings boomed. "Only so far as the pasture fence!"

Whirl: up he jumped, his wings chewed and loved the cool air. Before you'd say Uncle Einar Has Green Wings he sailed low across his farmland, trailing the clothes in a vast

from **"Uncle Einar"** by Ray Bradbury

fluttering loop through the pounding concussion and back-wash of his wings!

"Catch!"

Back from the trip, he sailed the clothes, dry as popcorn, down on a series of clean blankets she'd spread for their landing.

"Thank you!" she cried.

"Gahh!" he shouted, and flew off under the apple tree to brood.

●◆ What imaginary characteristics does Bradbury give Uncle Einar? What real-world characteristics does Uncle Einar have?

Imaginary	Real-World

●◆ Imagine Uncle Einar's wings have become all tangled up in the branches of the apple tree. What will he say to his wife? Write the conversation that takes place between the two. Use your notes about the characters to help you write the conversation.

Fantasy writers often create characters that are both realistic and fantastic at the same time.

In a fantasy, the author creates an imaginary world and then asks readers to believe that this world exists. The same thing happens in science fiction with one important difference: in a science fiction story, the writer spends a lot of time on issues that relate to science and technology. While a fantasy story might focus on a cat with wings, subjects for a science fiction story might include space colonies on Mars or robots that can reason.

When Bradbury writes science fiction, he performs the same kind of juggling act as when he writes fantasy. One place that you can clearly see Bradbury juggling the imaginary world and the real world is in his settings. (**Setting** is the time and place of a story.) As you read "Ylla," an excerpt from *The Martian Chronicles*, take note of Bradbury's setting. Underline any clues you find about time and place. What's real and what's imaginary?

← Response notes

206

"Ylla" from *The Martian Chronicles* by Ray Bradbury

They had a house of crystal pillars on the planet Mars by the edge of an empty sea, and every morning you could see Mrs. K eating the golden fruits that grew from the crystal walls, or cleaning the house with handfuls of magnetic dust which, taking all dirt with it, blew away on the hot wind. Afternoons, when the fossil sea was warm and motionless, and the wine trees stood stiff in the yard, and the little distant Martian bone town was all enclosed, and no one drifted out their doors, you could see Mr. K himself in his room, reading from a metal book with raised hieroglyphs over which he brushed his hand, as one might play a harp. And from the book, as his fingers stroked, a voice sang, a soft ancient voice, which told tales of when the sea was red steam on the shore and ancient men had carried clouds of metal insects and electric spiders into battle.

Mr. and Mrs. K had lived by the dead sea for twenty years, and their ancestors had lived in the same house, which turned and followed the sun, flower-like, for ten centuries.

Mr. and Mrs. K were not old. They had the fair, brownish skin of the true Martian, the yellow coin eyes, the soft musical voices. Once they had liked painting pictures with chemical fire, swimming in the canals in the seasons when the wine trees filled them with green liquors, and talking into the dawn together by the blue phosphorous portraits in the speaking room.

They were not happy now.

This morning Mrs. K stood between the pillars, listening to

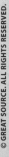

"Ylla" from ***The Martian Chronicles*** by Ray Bradbury

Response notes

the desert sands heat, melt into yellow wax, and seemingly run on the horizon.

Something was going to happen.

She waited.

She watched the blue sky of Mars as if it might at any moment grip in on itself, contract, and expel a shining miracle down upon the sand.

●◆Write a brief description of the setting for "Ylla." Then draw the story's setting. Use markers, crayons, or colored pencils to create a scene that reflects Bradbury's imaginary world.

207

When you read science fiction, notice how the author blends real and imaginary elements to create the setting.

Three
Bradbury's Plots

In addition to being an expert in developing setting and character, Ray Bradbury is a master at developing plot. **Plot** is the action of a story. It is the series of incidents that grow or build as the story develops. Bradbury's plots move back and forth between the real and the imaginary. This keeps his readers guessing about what will happen next.

Read the first part of Bradbury's short story "Fever Dream." Each time Bradbury switches between real and imaginary, make a note in the margin that looks like this: R ⟶ I. Each time he moves from the imaginary to the real, make a note like this: I ⟶ R.

← Response notes

"Fever Dream" by Ray Bradbury

They put him between fresh, clean, laundered sheets and there was always a newly squeezed glass of thick orange juice on the table under the dim pink lamp. All Charles had to do was call and Mom or Dad would stick their heads into his room to see how sick he was. The acoustics of the room were fine; you could hear the toilet gargling its porcelain throat of mornings, you could hear rain tap the roof or sly mice run in the secret walls or the canary singing in its cage downstairs. If you were very alert, sickness wasn't too bad.

He was thirteen, Charles was. It was mid-September, with the land beginning to burn with autumn. He lay in the bed for three days before the terror overcame him.

His hand began to change. His right hand. He looked at it and it was hot and sweating there on the counterpane alone. It fluttered, it moved a bit. Then it lay there, changing color.

That afternoon the doctor came again and tapped his thin chest like a little drum. "How are you?" asked the doctor, smiling. "I know, don't tell me: 'My *cold* is fine, Doctor, but *I* feel awful!' Ha!" He laughed at his own oft-repeated joke.

Charles lay there and for him that terrible and ancient jest was becoming a reality. The joke fixed itself in his mind. His mind touched and drew away from it in a pale terror. The doctor did not know how cruel he was with his jokes! "Doctor," whispered Charles, lying flat and colorless. "My *hand*, it doesn't *belong* to me any more. This morning it *changed* into something else. I want you to change it back, Doctor, Doctor!"

The doctor showed his teeth and patted his hand. "It looks fine to me, son. You just had a little fever dream."

"But it changed, Doctor, oh, Doctor," cried Charles, pitifully holding up his pale wild hand. "It *did!*"

The doctor winked. "I'll give you a pink pill for that." He

"Fever Dream" by Ray Bradbury

Response notes

popped a tablet onto Charles' tongue. "Swallow!"

"Will it make my hand change back and become *me*, again?"

"Yes, yes."

The house was silent when the doctor drove off down the road in his car under the quiet, blue September sky. A clock ticked far below in the kitchen world. Charles lay looking at his hand.

It did not change back. It was still something else.

The wind blew outside. Leaves fell against the cool window.

At four o'clock his other hand changed. It seemed almost to become a fever. It pulsed and shifted, cell by cell. It beat like a warm heart. The fingernails turned blue and then red. It took about an hour for it to change and when it was finished, it looked just like any ordinary hand. But it was not ordinary. It no longer was him any more. He lay in a fascinated horror and then fell into an exhausted sleep.

Mother brought the soup up at six. He wouldn't touch it. "I haven't any hands," he said, eyes shut.

"Your hands are perfectly good," said Mother.

"No," he wailed. "My hands are gone. I feel like I have stumps. Oh, Mama, Mama, hold me, hold me, I'm scared!"

She had to feed him herself.

"Mama," he said, "get the doctor, please, again. I'm so sick."

"The doctor'll be here tonight at eight," she said, and went out.

At seven, with night dark and close around the house, Charles was sitting up in bed when he felt the thing happening to first one leg and then the other. "Mama! Come quick!" he screamed.

But when Mama came the thing was no longer happening.

When she went downstairs, he simply lay without fighting as his legs beat and beat, grew warm, red-hot, and the room filled with the warmth of his feverish change. The glow crept up from his toes to his ankles and then to his knees.

"May I come in?" The doctor smiled in the doorway.

"Doctor!" cried Charles. "Hurry, take off my blankets!"

The doctor lifted the blankets tolerantly. "There you are. Whole and healthy. Sweating, though. A little fever. I told you not to move around, bad boy." He pinched the moist pink cheek. "Did the pills help? Did your hand change back?"

"No, no, now it's my other hand and my legs!"

"Well, well, I'll have to give you three more pills, one for each limb, eh, my little peach?" laughed the doctor.

"Will they help me? Please, please. What've I *got*?"

"A mild case of scarlet fever, complicated by a slight cold."

"Is it a germ that lives and has more little germs in me?"

"Yes."

"Are you *sure* it's scarlet fever? You haven't taken any tests!"

"I guess I know a certain fever when I see one," said the doctor, checking the boy's pulse with cool authority.

Charles lay there, not speaking until the doctor was crisply packing his black kit. Then in the silent room, the boy's voice made a small, weak pattern, his eyes alight with remembrance. "I read a book once. About petrified trees, wood turning to stone. About how trees fell and rotted and minerals got in and built up and they look just like trees, but they're not, they're stone." He stopped. In the quiet warm room his breathing sounded.

"Well?" asked the doctor.

"I've been thinking," said Charles after a time. "Do germs ever get big? I mean, in biology class they told us about one-celled animals, amoebas and things, and how millions of years ago they got together until there was a bunch and they made the first body. And more and more cells got together and got bigger and then finally maybe there was a fish and finally here *we* are, and all we are is a bunch of cells that decided to get together, to help each other out. Isn't that right?" Charles wet his feverish lips.

"What's all this about?" The doctor bent over him.

"I've got to tell you this. Doctor, oh, I've got to!" he cried. "What would happen, oh just pretend, please pretend, that just like in the old days, a lot of microbes got together and wanted to make a bunch, and reproduced and made *more*—"

His white hands were on his chest now, crawling toward his throat.

"And they decided to *take over* a person!" cried Charles.

"Take over a person?"

"Yes, *become* a person. *Me*, my hands, my feet! What if a disease somehow knew how to kill a person and yet live after him?"

He screamed.

The hands were on his neck.

The doctor moved forward, shouting.

➥ What do you think of "Fever Dream" so far?

....

....

....

....

210

●◆ Use the plot line below to take a closer look at how Bradbury develops his plot up to this point. Starting at the bottom, jot down notes about the incidents in "Fever Dream" that lead up to the story's climax. Note whether each incident is real (R) or imaginary (I).

Charles thinks the disease is trying to take over his body. (I)

211

Charles is in bed with a fever. (R)

●◆ Use your plot line to try to predict what will happen next in "Fever Dream."

Examining how writers of science fiction and fantasy move back and forth between the real and imaginary world can help you make predictions about story events.

Bradbury's Themes

Many science fiction and fantasy writers focus on one or two themes that they explore over and over again. (A story's **theme** is the generalization or observation the author makes about life or human nature.) One of Bradbury's favorite themes has to do with the crazy things that can happen when a real world and an imaginary world collide.

As you read the second half of "Fever Dream," circle words, phrases, and sentences that relate to the idea of worlds colliding.

Response notes

Does he??

212

"Fever Dream" (continued) by Ray Bradbury

At nine o'clock the doctor was escorted out to his car by the mother and father, who handed him his bag. They conversed in the cool night wind for a few minutes. "Just be sure his hands are kept strapped to his legs," said the doctor. "I don't want him hurting himself."

"Will he be all right, Doctor?" The mother held to his arm a moment.

He patted her shoulder. "Haven't I been your family physician for thirty years? It's the fever. He imagines things."

"But those bruises on his throat, he almost choked himself."

"Just you keep him strapped; he'll be all right in the morning."

The car moved off down the dark September road.

At three in the morning, Charles was still awake in his small black room. The bed was damp under his head and his back. He was very warm. Now he no longer had any arms or legs, and his body was beginning to change. He did not move on the bed, but looked at the vast blank ceiling space with insane concentration. For a while he had screamed and thrashed, but now he was weak and hoarse from it, and his mother had gotten up a number of times to soothe his brow with a wet towel. Now he was silent, his hands strapped to his legs.

He felt the walls of his body change, the organs shift, the lungs catch fire like burning bellows of pink alcohol. The room was lighted up as with the flickerings of a hearth.

Now he had no body. It was all gone. It was under him, but it was filled with a vast pulse of some burning, lethargic drug. It was as if a guillotine had neatly lopped off his head, and his head lay shining on a midnight pillow while the body, below, still alive, belonged to somebody else. The disease had eaten his body and from the eating had reproduced itself in feverish duplicate.

There were the little hand hairs and the fingernails and the scars and the toenails and the tiny mole on his right hip, all done again in perfect fashion.

"Fever Dream" (continued) by Ray Bradbury

Response notes

I am dead, he thought. I've been killed, and yet I live. My body is dead, it is all disease and nobody will know. I will walk around and it will not be me, it will be something else. It will be something all bad, all evil, so big and so evil it's hard to understand or think about. Something that will buy shoes and drink water and get married some day maybe and do more evil in the world than has ever been done.

Now the warmth was stealing up his neck, into his cheeks, like a hot wine. His lips burned, his eyelids, like leaves, caught fire. His nostrils breathed out blue flame, faintly, faintly.

This will be all, he thought. It'll take my head and my brain and fix each eye and every tooth and all the marks in my brain, and every hair and every wrinkle in my ears, and there'll be nothing left of me.

He felt his brain fill with a boiling mercury. He felt his left eye clench in upon itself and, like a snail, withdraw, shift. He was blind in his left eye. It no longer belonged to him. It was enemy territory. His tongue was gone, cut out. His left cheek was numbed, lost. His left ear stopped hearing. It belonged to someone else now. This thing that was being born, this mineral thing replacing the wooden log, this disease replacing healthy animal cell.

He tried to scream and he was able to scream loud and high and sharply in the room, just as his brain flooded down, his right eye and right ear were cut out, he was blind and deaf, all fire, all terror, all panic, all death.

His scream stopped before his mother ran through the door to his side.

It was a good, clear morning, with a brisk wind that helped carry the doctor up the path before the house. In the window above, the boy stood, fully dressed. He did not wave when the doctor waved and called, "What's this? Up? My God!"

The doctor almost ran upstairs. He came gasping into the bedroom.

"What are you doing out of bed?" he demanded of the boy. He tapped his thin chest, took his pulse and temperature. "Absolutely amazing! Normal. Normal, by God!"

"I shall never be sick again in my life," declared the boy, quietly, standing there, looking out the wide window. "Never."

"I hope not. Why, you're looking fine, Charles."

"Doctor?"

"Yes, Charles?"

"Can I go to school *now*?" asked Charles.

"Tomorrow will be time enough. You sound positively eager."

"I am. I like school. All the kids. I want to play with them and wrestle with them, and spit on them and play with the girls' pigtails and shake the teacher's hand, and rub my hands

213

on all the cloaks in the cloakroom, and I want to grow up and travel and shake hands with people all over the world, and be married and have lots of children, and go to libraries and handle books and—*all* of that I want to!" said the boy, looking off into the September morning. "What's the name you called me?"

"What?" The doctor puzzled. "I called you nothing but Charles."

"It's better than no name at all, I guess." The boy shrugged.

"I'm glad you want to go back to school," said the doctor.

"I really anticipate it," smiled the boy. "Thank you for your help, Doctor. Shake hands."

"Glad to."

They shook hands gravely, and the clear wind blew through the open window. They shook hands for almost a minute, the boy smiling up at the old man and thanking him.

Then, laughing, the boy raced the doctor downstairs and out to his car. His mother and father followed for the happy farewell.

"Fit as a fiddle!" said the doctor. "Incredible!"

"And strong," said the father. "He got out of his straps himself during the night. Didn't you, Charles?"

"Did I?" said the boy.

"You did! How?"

"Oh," the boy said, "that was a long time ago."

"A long time ago!"

They all laughed, and while they were laughing, the quiet boy moved his bare foot on the sidewalk and merely touched, brushed against a number of red ants that was scurrying about on the sidewalk. Secretly, his eyes shining, while his parents chatted with the old man, he saw the ants hesitate, quiver, and lie still on the cement. He sensed they were cold now.

"Good-by!"

The doctor drove away, waving.

The boy walked ahead of his parents. As he walked he looked away toward the town and began to hum "School Days" under his breath.

"It's good to have him well again," said the father.

"Listen to him. He's so looking forward to school!"

The boy turned quietly. He gave each of his parents a crushing hug. He kissed them both several times.

Then without a word he bounded up the steps into the house.

In the parlor, before the others entered, he quickly opened the bird cage, thrust his hand in, and petted the yellow canary, *once.*

Then he shut the cage door, stood back, and waited.

➥ Bradbury often examines what can happen when real and imaginary worlds collide. In "Fever Dream," what *does* happen? Write a summary of the second part of the story.

➥ You can use the events of the story to infer the story's **theme**. To do this, ask yourself: "What's the point of what happens? What's this story all about?" Write your theme statement here.

215

➥ What are your thoughts about this theme? Do you agree with it? Explain.

Just like all fiction, science fiction and fantasy stories have themes. To find them, ask yourself, "What's it all about?"

How does Bradbury come up with his imaginary worlds? Where does he get his fantastic ideas? People have asked Bradbury these questions for years. In the introduction to his book *S Is for Space*, he tries to explain. Read Bradbury's introduction with a pen in hand. Underline or **highlight** each source of inspiration Bradbury names.

Response notes

introduction to *S Is for Space* by Ray Bradbury

Jules Verne was my father.

H. G. Wells was my wise uncle.

Edgar Allan Poe was the batwinged cousin we kept high in the back attic room.

Flash Gordon and Buck Rogers were my brothers and friends.

There you have my ancestry.

Adding, of course, the fact that in all probability Mary Wollstonecraft Shelley, author of *Frankenstein*, was my mother.

With a family like that, how else could I have turned out than as I did: a writer of fantasy and most curious tales of science fiction.

I lived up in the trees with Tarzan a good part of my life with my hero Edgar Rice Burroughs. When I swung down out of the foliage I asked for a toy typewriter during my twelfth year, at Christmas. On this rattletrap machine I wrote my first John Carter, Warlord of Mars, imitation sequels, and from memory tapped out whole episodes of *Chandu the Magician*.

I sent away boxtops and think I joined every secret radio society that existed. I saved comic strips, most of which I still have in great boxes down in my California basement. I went to movie matinees. I devoured the works of H. Rider Haggard and Robert Louis Stevenson.

In the midst of my young summers I leapt high and dove deep down into the vast ocean of Space, long long before the Space Age itself was more than a fly speck on the two-hundred-inch Mount Palomar telescope.

In other words, I was in love with everything I did. My heart did not beat, it exploded. I did not warm toward a subject, I boiled over. I have always run fast and yelled loud about a list of great and magical things I knew I simply could not live without.

I was a beardless boy-magician who pulled irritable rabbits out of papier-mâché hats. I became a bearded man-magician who pulled rockets out of his typewriter and out of a Star Wilderness that stretched as far as eye and mind could see and imagine.

216

introduction to **S Is for Space** by Ray Bradbury

← Response notes →

My enthusiasm stood me well over the years. I have never tired of the rockets and the stars. I never cease enjoying the good fun of scaring heck out of myself with some of my weirder, darker, tales.

So here in this new collection of stories you will find not only *S is for Space*, but a series of subtitles that might well read *D is for Dark*, or *T is for Terrifying*, or *D is for Delight*. Here you will find just about every side of my nature and my life that you might wish to discover. My ability to laugh out loud with the sheer discovery that I am alive in a strange, wild, and exhilarating world. My equally great ability to jump and raise up a crop of goosepimples when I smell strange mushrooms growing in my cellar at midnight, or hear a spider fiddling away at his tapestry-web in the closet just before sunrise.

You who read, and I who write, are very much the same. The young person locked away in me has dared to write these stories for your pleasure. We meet on the common ground of an uncommon Age, and share out our gifts of dark and light, good dream and bad, simple joy and not so simple sorrow.

The boy-magician speaks from another year. I stand aside and let him say what he most needs to say. I listen and enjoy.

I hope you will, too.

217

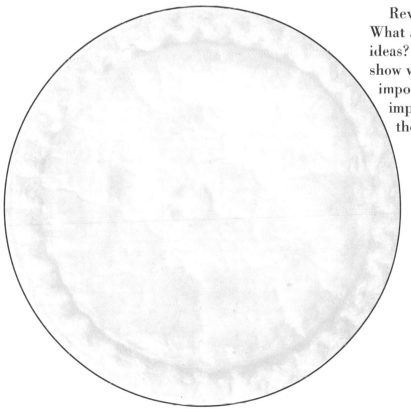

Review Bradbury's introduction. What are some of the sources for his ideas? Use the pie chart below to show which sources were most important and which were least important. (The bigger the wedge, the more important the source.)

You've been chosen to create a cover for the official Ray Bradbury biography. Your editor has given you instructions to create a cover that captures the "essence" of Bradbury. Use the space below to

1. draw a sketch for the book's cover that reflects Bradbury's imaginary worlds, and
2. write a blurb for the cover that describes Bradbury and his writing.

Understanding the sources that inspire a writer can help you better understand his or her work.

10 Excerpt from "The Computer Date", from *A Summer Life* by Gary Soto. Copyright © 1990 by University Press of New England.

11,13,16 "Seventh Grade" from *Baseball in April* by Gary Soto. Copyright © 1990 by Gary Soto. Reprinted by permission of Harcourt Brace & Company.

20 "Oranges" from *New and Selected Poems* by Gary Soto. Copyright © 1995. Published by Chronicle Books, San Francisco.

24 "One More Time" from *Living Up the Street* by Gary Soto (Dell, 1992). Copyright © 1985 by Gary Soto. Used by permission of the author.

28, 29 From *The Diary of Latoya Hunter* by Latoya Hunter. Copyright © 1992 by Latoya Hunter. Reprinted by permission of Crown Publishers, Inc.

32 "Playgrounds of the Future" from *Newsweek*, May 12, 1997. Copyright © 1997, Newsweek, Inc. All rights reserved. Reprinted by permission.

36 " A Time to Talk" from *The Poety of Robert Frost*, edited by Edward Connery Lathem. Copyright 1936, 1951 by Robert Frost, © 1964 by Lesley Frost Ballantine, Copyright 1923, © 1969 by Henry Holt and Company, Inc., © 1997 by Edward Connery Lathem. Reprinted by permission of Henry Holt and Company, Inc.

45 From *So Far from the Bamboo Grove* by Yoko Kawashima Watkins. Copyright © 1986 by Yoko Kawashima Watkins. By permission of Lothrop, Lee & Shepard Books, a division of William Morrow & Company, Inc.

48 "The Dinner Party" by Mona Gardner. Reprinted by permission of *The Saturday Review*. Copyright © 1978, General Media Communications, Inc.

54 "Hero on the Ball Field" by Robert W. Peterson from *Boy's Life* (April 1997). Reprinted by permission of Boy Scouts of America and Robert W. Peterson.

58 From *I Never Had It Made* by Jackie Robinson, as told to Alfred Duckett. Copyright © 1995 by Rachel Robinson. Reprinted by permission of The Ecco Press.

62 Excerpt, pages 25-26 from *Stealing Home* by Sharon Robinson. Copyright © 1996 by Sharon Robinson. Reprinted by permission of HarperCollins Publishers.

65 Lucille Clifton: "Jackie Robinson." Copyright © 1987 by Lucille Clifton. Reprinted from *Good Woman: Poems and a Memoir 1969-1980* with the permission of BOA Editions, Ltd., 260 East Ave. Rochester NY 1464.

70 "knoxville, tennessee" from *Black Feeling, Black Talk, Black Judgement* by Nikki Giovanni. Copyright © 1968, 1970 by Nikki Giovanni. By permission of William Morrow & Company, Inc.

73 "Graduation Morning" from *Chants* by Pat Mora. Reprinted with permission from the publisher of *Chants* (Houston: Arte Publico Press—University of Houston, 1985)

75 "Mother to Son" from *Collected Poems* by Langston Hughes. Copyright © 1994 by the Estate of Langston Hughes. Reprinted by permission of Alfred A. Knopf, Inc.

77 "Birthday Box" by Jane Yolen. Copyright © 1995 by Jane Yolen. First appeared in *Birthday Surprises: Ten Great Stories to Unwrap*, published by Morrow Junior Books. Reprinted by permission of Curtis Brown, Ltd.

84 From *Don't Sweat the Small Stuff: Simple Ways to Keep the Little Things from Taking Over Your Life* by Richard Carlson, Ph.D. Copyright © 1997, Richard Carlson, Ph.D. Reprinted with permission by Hyperion.

89 From *Frontier* by Louis L'Amour. Photographs by David Muench. Copyright © 1984 by Louis L'Amour Enterprises, Inc. Used by permission of Bantam Books, a division of Bantam Doubleday Dell Publishing Group, Inc.

98 "The Princess of Light" from *The Dancing Kettle and Other Japanese Folktales* retold by Yoshiko Uchida, illustrated by Richard C. Jones. Reprinted with permission.

102 From *The Forever Christmas Tree* by Yoshiko Uchida. Reprinted with permission.

102 From *The Invisible Thread* by Yoshiko Uchida. Reprinted with the permission of Simon & Schuster Books for Young Readers, an imprint of Simon & Schuster Children's Publishing Division. Copyright © 1991 Yoshiko Uchida.

105 From *Journey Home* by Yoshiko Uchida. Reprinted with the permission of Margaret K. McElderry Books, an imprint of Simon & Schuster Children's Publishing Division. Text copyright © 1978 Yoshiko Uchida.

108 From *Desert Exile: The Uprooting of a Japanese-American Family* by Yoshiko Uchida. First published by University of Washington Press, 1982. Reprinted with permission.

111 From conversation with Yoshiko Uchida. Reprinted with permission.

114 "Turkeys" from B. White, *Mama Makes Up Her Mind* (pages 12-16). Copyright © 1993 by Bailey White. Reprinted by permission of Addison Wesley Longman.

118, 122 "Charles" from *The Lottery* by Shirley Jackson. Copyright © 1948, 1949 by Shirley Jackson, and copyright renewed © 1976, 1977 by Laurence Hyman, Barry Hyman, Mrs. Sarah Webster and Mrs. Joanne Schnurer. Reprinted by permission of Farrar, Straus & Giroux, Inc.

125 "The King and the Shirt", from *Fables and Fairy Tales* by Leo Tolstoy, translated by Ann Dunnigan. Translation copyright © 1962 by Ann Dunnigan; Foreward copyright © by New American Library. Used by permission of Dutton Signet, a division of Penguin Putnam Inc.

130, 133 From *Volcano* by Patricia Lauber. Reprinted with the permission of Simon & Schuster Books for Young Readers, an imprint of Simon & Schuster Children's Publishing Division. Copyright © 1986 Patricia Lauber.

136 From *On the Road with Charles Kuralt* by Charles Kuralt. Reprinted by permission of The Putnam Publishing Group. Copyright © 1985 by CBS Inc.

142 From "A Sea Worry" by Maxine Hong Kingston. Copyright © 1978 by Maxine Hong Kingston. Reprinted by permission of the author.

146, 150 "Shells" from *Every Living Thing* by Cynthia Rylant. Reprinted with the permission of Simon & Schuster Books for Young Readers, an imprint of Simon & Schuster Children's Publishing Division. Copyright © 1985 Cynthia Rylant.

155 From "Ta-Na-E-Ka" by Mary Whitebird in *Scholastic Voice*, December 13, 1973. Copyright © 1973 by Scholastic Inc. Reprinted by permission.

158 From *Dragonwings* by Laurence Yep. Copyright © 1975 by Laurence Yep. Used by permission of HarperCollins Publishers.

163 Excerpt from *Island of the Blue Dolphins*. Copyright © 1960, renewed 1988 by Scott O'Dell. Reprinted by permission of Houghton Mifflin Company. All rights reserved.

219

166 "Chinese Hot Pot" from *Expounding the Doubtful Points* by Wing Tek Lum. Copyright © 1987 by Wing Tek Lum. Reprinted by permission of the author.

168 "The Inspector-General" from *The Sneeze* by Anton Chekhov, translated by Michael Frayn; published by Methuen. Reprinted by permission of Random House UK, Ltd.

172 "Direction" by Alonzo Lopez, from *Whispering Wind* by Terry Allen. Copyright © 1972 by the Institute of American Indian Arts. Used by permission of Doubleday, a division of Bantam Doubleday Dell Publishing Group, Inc.

176 "The Funeral" from *Whispers of Intimate Things* by Gordon Parks. Copyright © 1971 by Gordon Parks. Used by permission of Viking Penguin, a division of Penguin Putnam Inc.

178 "There's This That I Like About Hockey, My Lad" by John Kieran. Reprinted with the permission of Simon & Schuster from *The American Sporting Scene* by John Kieran. Copyright 1941 by John Kieran and Joseph Golinkin, copyright renewed © 1988 by John Kieran.

183 "Cynthia in the Snow" by Gwendolyn Brooks. Copyright © 1956 by Gwendolyn Brooks Blakely. Used by permission of HarperCollins Publishers.

185 "Chrysalis Diary" by Paul Fleischman. Text copyright © 1988 by Paul Fleischman. Illustrations copyright © 1988 by Eric Beddows. Used by permission of HarperCollins Publishers.

190 "Our Juvenile Curfew Is Working" by New Orleans Mayor Marc H. Morial. Editorial originally appeared in *The Washington Post*, January 6, 1995. Used by permission of the author.

195 From "Titanic Review" by Roger Ebert from *Chicago Sun-Times*. Copyright © 1997 Chicago Sun-Times Inc. Used with permission of Roger Ebert.

198, 200 "Homeless" from *Living Out Loud* by Anna Quindlen. Copyright © 1987 by Anna Quindlen. Reprinted by permission of Random House, Inc.

204 From "Uncle Einar" by Ray Bradbury. Reprinted by permission of Don Congdon Associates, Inc. Copyright © 1947, renewed 1975 by Ray Bradbury.

206 From *The Martian Chronicles* by Ray Bradbury. Reprinted by permission of Don Congdon Associates, Inc. Copyright © 1949, renewed 1977 by Ray Bradbury.

208, 212 "Fever Dream" by Ray Bradbury. Reprinted by permission of Don Congdon Associates, Inc. Copyright © 1948, renewed 1975 by Ray Bradbury.

216 From *S Is for Space* by Ray Bradbury. Reprinted by permission of Don Congdon Associates, Inc. Copyright © 1966, renewed 1994 by Ray Bradbury.

Design: Christine Ronan Design

Front and Back Cover Photographs: Mel Hill

Interior Photographs: Unless otherwise noted below, all photographs are the copyrighted work of Mel Hill.
9 © Loren Santow/Ibid, Inc.
27 © Hulton-Deutsch Collection/Corbis
39 © SuperStock International
55 © Patrisha Thomson/Tony Stone Images
69 © Doug Plummer/Photonica
83 © Deborah Raven/Photonica
97 © Brian Bailey/Tony Stone Images
113 © Jack Hutcheson/Photonica
129 © Eric Horan/Gamma Liason International
145 © Hulton-Deutsch Collection/Corbis
161 © Tom Craig/FPG International
175 © Keith Brofsky/Tony Stone Images
189 © Nick Vaccaro/Photonica
203 © H. Horenstein/Photonica

Every effort has been made to secure complete rights and permissions for each literary excerpt presented herein. Updated acknowledgments, if needed, will appear in subsequent printings.

Picture Research: Feldman and Associates

Glossary

alliteration, the repetition of the same consonant sound at the beginning of words.

antagonist, the character in fiction or drama who is a rival or opponent of the PROTAGONIST.

assonance, the repetition of vowel sounds across syllables or words. Assonance is a characteristic of POETRY.

audience, those people who read or hear what a writer has written.

author's perspective, a way of looking at a subject or a work of literature. An author's perspective can be influenced by background knowledge and experiences.

author's purpose, the reason why an author writes. Authors write to entertain, to inform or explain, to persuade or argue, or to express personal thoughts or feelings.

autobiography, an author's account of his or her own life.

bias, favoring (and often presenting) one side of an argument.

biography, the story of a person's life written by another person.

cause and effect, a relationship that exists when one event (the cause) brings about the other event (the effect).

characterization, the method an author uses to reveal or describe CHARACTERS and their various personalities and motives.

characters, people, animals, or imaginary creatures in a story.

conflict, the problem or struggle in a story that triggers the action. Conflict can be external (a character facing society, another character, or a physical challenge) or internal (a character facing opposing forces within him- or herself).

connotation, the emotional meaning of a word in addition to its dictionary meaning.

consonance, the repetition of consonant sounds across syllables or words. Consonance is a characteristic of POETRY.

denotation, the exact, "dictionary" definition of a word.

description, writing that paints a colorful picture of a person, place, thing, or idea using concrete, vivid DETAILS.

details, words from a description that elaborate on subjects, characters, or action in a work. Sensory details are generally vivid, colorful, and appeal to the senses.

dialogue, the talking that goes on between CHARACTERS in a story.

drama, a GENRE or form of literature meant to be performed by actors before an audience. Drama tells its story through action and DIALOGUE. Dramas are also known as plays.

expository nonfiction, writing that explains FACTS and ideas.

fact, something that can be proven to be true.

fiction, writing that tells an imaginary story.

figurative language, language used to create a special effect or feeling. Figurative language goes beyond the literal meanings of the words used. SIMILE, METAPHOR, and PERSONIFICATION are examples of figurative language.

221

free verse, poetry that does not have a regular METER or RHYME scheme.

generalize, to take specific information and apply it to gain a broad, general insight.

genre, a category or type of literature based on its style, form, and content. The major genres are FICTION, NONFICTION, DRAMA, and POETRY.

highlight, to underline, circle, or mark the information that is most important as you read.

imagery, the words or phrases a writer uses to describe or present objects, feelings, actions, ideas, etc. Imagery is usually based on SENSORY LANGUAGE.

inference, a reasonable guess based upon information provided in a piece of writing.

irony (situational), the contrast between what characters or readers might reasonably expect to happen and what actually happens.

journal, a daily record of thoughts, impressions, and autobiographical information. A journal can be a source for ideas about writing.

main idea, the central point or purpose in a piece of NONFICTION.

metaphor, comparison of two unlike things without using a word of comparison such as *like* or *as*. Example: "The stars were diamonds."

meter, a poem's RHYTHM.

mood, the feeling(s) a story gives readers. Examples: happy, peaceful, sad.

narrative nonfiction, writing that tells a true story about people, places, or events.

narrator, the writer or speaker who tells the story or describes events in the story.

nonfiction, writing that tells a true story or explores an idea. There are many categories of nonfiction, including autobiography, biography, and essay.

objective, NONFICTION writing that relates information in an impersonal manner; without feelings or opinions.

omniscient NARRATOR, a third-person narrator who is able to see into the minds of all the characters in a literary work, narrating the story from multiple POINTS OF VIEW.

onomatopoeia, using words that sound like what they mean. Examples: *buzz, crackle, hiss*.

opinion, a person's personal ideas about a subject. An opinion cannot be proven true or false.

personification, a form of FIGURATIVE LANGUAGE in which an idea, object, or animal is given human characteristics. Example: "The rock stubbornly refused to move."

perspective, See POINT OF VIEW.

persuasion, writing that is meant to change the way the reader thinks or acts.

plot, the action or sequence of events in a story.

poetry, an imaginative kind of writing that tells a story, describes an experience, or reflects on an idea. It is usually characterized by STANZAS rather than paragraphs; it uses RHYTHM, FIGURATIVE LANGUAGE, SENSORY LANGUAGE, and sometimes RHYME.

222

point of view, the angle from which a story is told. A first person point of view means that one of the characters is telling the story. Example: "I was angry when I left the shop, and I'm sure Leo was too." A third person point of view means that someone outside the story is telling it. "The two boys were angry when they left the shop."

predict, to use what you already know in order to guess what will happen in the future.

protagonist, the chief character in a work of fiction or drama.

repetition, a figure of speech in which a word, phrase, or idea is repeated for emphasis and effect in a piece of literature.

rhyme, the similarity of sound at the end of two or more words. Rhyme is a characteristic of POETRY.

rhythm, the ordered occurrence of sound in POETRY.

sensory language, language that appeals to the five senses: sight, sound, taste, smell, and touch.

sequence, the order of events.

setting, the time and place of a story.

short story, a brief fictional narrative.

simile, a comparison of two unlike objects using *like* or *as*. Example: "The sun rose like a giant flower out of the sky."

stanza, a group of lines that are set off to form a division in POETRY.

structure, the form or organization a writer uses for a literary work. There are a large number of possible forms, such as fable, parable, romance, satire, etc.

style, how an author uses words, phrases, and sentences to form his or her ideas.

summarize, to restate briefly the most important parts of a piece of writing in your own words.

symbol, an object, person, or event that stands for something else.

text structure, the way writing is organized.

theme, the statement about life or human nature that an author wants to make to the reader.

223

tone, the writer's attitude toward a subject. A writer's tone can be serious, sarcastic, objective, etc.

viewpoint, an author's opinion on a particular subject.

visualize, to see or picture in your mind what you read.

224